T0294775

PROJECT
RESTART

PROJECT
RESTART

From Prem to the Parks.
How Football Came Out of Lockdown.

JON BERRY

First published by Pitch Publishing, 2020

Pitch Publishing
A2 Yeoman Gate
Yeoman Way
Worthing
Sussex
BN13 3QZ
www.pitchpublishing.co.uk
info@pitchpublishing.co.uk

ISBN 978 1 78531 800 9

Typesetting and origination by Pitch Publishing

Printed and bound by Short Run Press Limited, Exeter, UK

Contents

This is for all those in the National Health Service and the care sector who have worked so bravely and selflessly and who continue to do so. This book is for you and for all those campaigning to keep these services free at the point of use and in public hands. Our biggest tribute would be to make sure you are all properly and fairly rewarded.

This is also for everyone who emptied the bins, delivered our post and parcels, stacked the shelves, got our medicines, carried on teaching our children and did all those jobs that we know now make them key workers.

And it's for those in the game – at every level – who kept their clubs afloat, worked in their communities and never failed to imagine that, somehow, we'd get some sort of football back again. The pandemic has taught us that football isn't that important, but maybe it's the most important of the unimportant things.

Maybe.

Foreword

We knew it shouldn't matter, but it did – a bit

I've always known that I lived in a society where there was unfairness, inequality and tragedy. All the same, for a long time, I didn't think I lived in one where something really, genuinely bad would happen to everyone.

Sure, we'd had those miserable climate warnings. For some, the UK winter of 2020 had already brought unbridled misery as persistent, torrential rain ruined properties and livelihoods. Doomsters had been warning us for some time that 'freak' weather could become the norm unless we changed our behaviour. It all seemed a bit distant, though. Stuff like that really wasn't going to affect our lives in the long term.

Pandemics? Shocking and tragic as they may have been, they happened in other countries whose authorities didn't have stuff under control like we had. And then it became horribly real.

Like almost every genuine football supporter I know, I frequently ask myself a question to which I don't know the answer: why do I let the game in general, and my team in particular, matter to me? For all the jokiness, you'll know what I mean – checking the score when you should be grinning happily at your niece's wedding; knowing that you'll be grumpy that evening if you've lost; flicking the remote from a major world event because you just need to know some entirely inconsequential scrap of football-related nonsense. Let's not even talk about planning holidays, arranging social events and skipping off work early.

In those first few shocking and unsettling weeks in March and April, we had to square up to what we'd always known: football really isn't that important in the face of real danger and disaster. The impact of Covid-19 was all-consuming and despite the foot-dragging of many of those in charge, it soon became plain that professional football, played in front of crowds of people, was an unthinkable folly.

All of which lasted for about three or four weeks, by which time it became acceptable to start asking what was going to happen to the beautiful game. With plenty of time for idle contemplation during lockdown, I became fascinated by how this whole process of restarting football was going to play out. In the pages that follow, I've tried to put together a living history of what happened, looking at football and its place in the wider world. At the centre of this are case studies of nine clubs operating at a range of levels. The choice was arbitrary other than trying to ensure that I got a spread of clubs from the Premier League to your local sports and social set-up.

Communicating with anyone from any of the fully professional clubs during the height of the pandemic was almost impossible. Attempts to set up online interviews, get a response to emails or find someone to answer the phone became a dispiriting business. In the lower leagues, many non-playing staff had been placed on furlough – a term which I don't think any of us had ever used in our lives before, but which became quickly installed as part of everyday conversation. Up at the top level, particularly as the restart became a fact of life, overstretched media teams became entirely inaccessible.

But there were – and are – plenty of other sources from which the temperature of the times could be taken. By trawling media – local and national – and loitering on forums and chat rooms, I've put together a picture that I hope will be familiar in many aspects to fans of all clubs. Eventually, I got to speak to quite a few key people: members of supporters' trusts and supporters' clubs; stalwarts of non-league football who do everything from maintaining the website to painting the goalposts; managers, chairmen, chief executives, academics and researchers.

At the core of this book are the chosen clubs, from the Premier League to the parks, but there is plenty of mention of other teams and you'll be able to find where yours features because a handy index is provided. My principal intention has been to paint a picture of what was happening in football but to do so I make no apology for looking at the game in the context of what was happening in society in general. In order to do that, I've had to engage in occasional political commentary. I haven't been so coy as to pretend any neutrality; you're at complete liberty to disagree with the opinions expressed and I've even furnished you with contact details at the end so that you can tell me why I'm such a fool to think as I do.

Much of this book was written in June and July. At that time, the only two leagues that were able to get back into full action were the Premier League and the Championship. Below that level, barring some play-off action, all we could do was wait and see and hope that, somehow, some sort of football would soon take place, not least so that some income could be generated and the employment of hundreds of people could become more secure. In this, especially below the top two levels, those who worked in football, in whatever capacity, were in the same boat as the rest of society.

One of the things we learnt during the pandemic was that the people who emptied our bins, stacked the shelves, drove the buses, worked at the pharmacy or delivered our post and parcels genuinely were those who kept us going. That's even before we get to those who cared for the elderly, tended the sick, nursed the terminally ill and worked until they were emotionally and physically drained. The pages that follow acknowledge that even though we were all trying to come to terms with a world turned on its head, it was just about permissible to strive for those things we knew were trivial: we're capable of carrying two ideas in our heads at once. We knew that it was possible to be respectful to those who had suffered while trying to grasp for some of the trifles that make life normal.

Footballers showed themselves as keen as anyone to demonstrate humility and a sense of perspective. Some went a great deal further than that. This book is written out of gratitude to the van driver as well as the star striker. Both remind us of what it is to be human.

Chapter 1

Lockdown. When we admitted it really was happening to us

I'll say it out loud. Football is important.

It's true that there are millions upon millions of people for whom it is a massive irrelevance. In many ways, people like me envy them. They go through life unburdened by anxiety about the performance of a bunch of athletes who wear laundry associated with their towns, cities and grandparents or who just happen to have made a simple, misguided fashion choice.

But for other millions, hundreds of millions in fact, football is important. I have no intention of dissecting arguments about it being a shield behind which men can hold conversations without having to reveal any true emotion: I have neither the expertise nor inclination to do so. Neither am I going to go down the road of bemoaning its utter capitulation to the ugly dollar, although it's impossible to avoid comment about how it has done so.

I'm starting from the simple, and simplistic, position that football is important and that when it disappeared in the early spring of 2020 in the UK, it sent a clear signal that Covid-19 was established as an unwelcome fact of our lives. What this book does is to look at how it came back to life at every level from the lumberers on the parks to the humblest of semi-pros to the glitterati of the Premier League.

Our individual partings with the game will differ, but on a personal note, it could not have been more typical. On Saturday, 7 March, my team, Birmingham City, managed to bring an unbeaten run of ten games (six of them were draws) to an end with a lame defeat at home to Reading. Nothing unusual here. A downcast journey home but not something that a couple of pints wouldn't soon cure. Goodness knows, flat, disappointing performances against mediocre opponents is the very stuff of life. Maybe next week would be better: the triumph of hope over experience is the badge of all true supporters. High-flying West Brom away. You never know.

That same weekend, up in the higher reaches of the Premier League, the giants battled it out for the delight and diversion of its worldwide audience. There seemed little to worry about. It's true that the government's committee for emergencies, COBRA, had met a couple of times, albeit not always graced by the presence of the Prime Minister, but his bumptious presence at the England–Wales rugby game reassured us all that there was nothing greatly amiss. The Cheltenham horse racing festival, attracting tens of thousands, was going ahead in the coming week and the city of Liverpool was about to welcome some 3,000 travelling fans from Madrid for a game on the evening of Wednesday 11th. On that same day, the Spanish government closed its schools and colleges and announced that the country had suffered 47 deaths from the virus – second only to Italy in terms of European fatalities. In the weeks that followed there was a spike in deaths related to Covid-19 on Merseyside by a factor of 3.5 in comparison with neighbouring areas. But the threat in those first days in March still seemed distant and remote.

By ten o'clock on the evening of Monday, 9 March, although we didn't know it at the time, the last ball had been kicked in the Premier League for three months as Leicester beat Aston Villa, aided by some truly comic defending and goalkeeping. Although Liverpool's game went ahead on the Wednesday, Arsenal's fixture against Manchester City, scheduled for the same day, was postponed. Some Arsenal players had been in contact with the owner of Olympiacos, Evangalos

Marinakis, who had contracted the disease and so this was deemed a sensible precaution – one that turned out to be rather more astute when it was announced next day that the Arsenal manager, Mikel Arteta, had also become infected. On Thursday, 12 March, Wolves went to Athens to play Olympiacos in a game played behind closed doors – and then that was that. Although some games were played in the National League, England's fifth tier, on Saturday, 14 March, football at the top level was put on hold by the end of the week as all fixtures were called off. At that point there was one recorded death caused by Covid-19 in the UK.

In the groundhog weeks that followed, the world became unrecognisable; we'll all harbour our own lessons and memories. The awful truth of lives lived precariously and dogged by disadvantage became evident to us all. This book is not the medium through which to comment on the utter hopelessness with which this was addressed by so many world leaders, but there is no doubting some of the crass incompetence which prevented any chance of early control over the virus. And yet, through it all, as the problems of wages, rents, businesses, education, social care and the health service held proper sway over public discourse, one question doggedly popped up like an irrelevant, irritating whack-a-mole: when will football start again? In fact, there was a range of ways that football found its way into public debate almost from the start of the crisis. Because it's important.

Footballers and their earnings are a constant source of outraged delight for us all. In what can only be a throwback to the game's working-class roots, their payment is always expressed as a weekly wage, somehow prompting the odd image of them having to line up on a Friday at the desk of the CEO who hands them their earnings in a square, brown envelope. Among fans, there is a grudging acceptance that those at the very top of the game might just merit the jaw-dropping sums that come their way, but that journeymen pros from Middle Europe should consider themselves bloody fortunate. Ever since the maximum wage (yes, younger readers, you read that right) was abolished and Johnny Haynes became the first £100-a-week footballer in 1961, the income of those who do nothing more than punt a ball about a field has been fair game for general disapproval, especially from those not infatuated with the beautiful game. For most players, however, the life-changing largesse of the stars is entirely unattainable; the early days of the virus made this startlingly clear.

Trawl through as much information as you can, and the business of nailing footballers' wages seems to be more art than science. Nevertheless, most reliable figures indicate that average weekly wages slope downwards from £50,000 in the Premier League to £11,000 in the

Championship (a figure distorted by relegated teams encumbered with top-level contractual obligations), £2,300 in the third division in League One and down to around £1,100 in the fourth. These figures reveal that there exists in society a very small group of talented young men who, as long as they behave prudently and are well advised, should never have to want for anything in their lives. Others should be able to establish networks and expertise that will allow them a comfortable future existence and others still have the opportunity to give themselves a leg-up for when they quit the professional game, probably in their mid-30s. Quite why it was that the Health Secretary, Matt Hancock, felt it necessary to single out this particular constituency, just as the seriousness of the situation crowded in on us like a dark fog, is something only he and his colleagues can answer.

On Thursday, 2 April the death toll in England had reached 561. However poor our maths may have been, we were becoming familiar with the notion of exponential growth and the critical importance of infection rates. Those who had not been paralysed by concern about their income and the welfare of loved ones found thousands of ways to contribute to the common good. A government scheme asking for volunteers was soon overwhelmed as over half a million people signed up. With all this going on, on 2 April Hancock chose to make this statement:

I think that everybody needs to play their part in this national effort and that means Premier League footballers too. Given the sacrifices that many people are making, including some of my colleagues in the NHS who have made the ultimate sacrifice of going in to work and have caught the disease and have sadly died, I think the first thing that Premier League footballers can do is make a contribution, take a pay cut and play their part.

I can't be certain, but my strong suspicion is that, unlike some major companies who operate on UK soil, footballers pay their taxes. It is also very well documented that many of them, particularly those from disadvantaged parts of the world, make huge contributions to their home communities. The same goes for dozens who support charities and foundations in the localities of their clubs. In those early weeks of lockdown, the conduct of some of the country's leading industrialists and entrepreneurs, who sat on their hands and asked for bailouts as their workers lay awake frantic with worry, went unremarked upon by government politicians. Footballers, on the other hand, got a special mention. Why? Because football is important.

Hancock's ill-advised observations drew justifiably irritated responses from players. Comments from

Newcastle's Danny Rose, who had already shown himself unafraid to speak out about racism in the game, were typical of the reaction of many of his colleagues: 'It was just not needed for people who are not involved in football trying to tell footballers what to do with their money.' It later emerged that Rose had already made a five-figure donation to a hospital that had previously treated him for injury.

On 5 April, Wayne Rooney in his *Sunday Times* column questioned the Health Secretary's motives with admirable incisiveness:

> *Not every footballer is in the same position. Yet suddenly the whole profession has been put on the spot with a demand for 30 per cent pay cuts across the board. Why are footballers suddenly the scapegoats? How the past few days have played out is a disgrace. He [Hancock] was supposed to be giving the nation the latest on the biggest crisis we've faced in our lifetimes. Why was the pay of footballers even in his head? Was he desperate to divert attention from his Government's handling of this pandemic?*

In yet another instance in the crisis of government ministers stubbornly failing to consult people who may actually know something, Hancock would have been better served if he'd made himself aware of what was happening beyond his narrow experience. Liverpool's Jordan Henderson had already approached captains in the top flight to coordinate an initiative to take pay cuts and contribute to NHS funding. Within days of his doing so, representatives of the English Football League (the body charged with oversight of the three divisions below the Premier League) worked towards a voluntary agreement whereby players would defer some of their wages for April – with a telling exemption for those whose earnings were a world away from the stratospheric payments of screaming headlines.

Before any of this had happened, Gary Neville had closed his two Manchester hotels to the public and opened them to NHS workers free of charge. There were no staff redundancies in either establishment.

The contrast between his actions and those of some of the owners of Premier League clubs was stark. Even before Hancock's comments, Newcastle had placed all non-playing staff on furlough, shortly to be followed by Liverpool and Tottenham. In the case of the latter, the revelation that the owner, Daniel Levy, had been awarded a £3 million bonus for completing the new stadium on time – it was very late – served to further increase the ire of the supporters' groups who became instrumental in the decision to reverse the move. In Liverpool the voice of supporters also prevailed. In

Newcastle, Mike Ashley, that very model of the modern entrepreneur, remained resolute, holding out on a decision – despite pleas from the players – until the club had been sold to a Saudi-backed conglomerate (spoiler alert – the sale fell through). The views of Matt Hancock on the actions of these owners does not seem to be a matter of public record.

Even as the numbers of deaths began to be measured in thousands, concern about the future of all professional sport took root in public discourse. Would the current season finish? If so, how would that be arranged? Might there be something morally questionable about considering such arrangements when some nurses were still making face masks out of old flannels and kitchen roll? On talk shows and empty rolling-news sports bulletins, most pundits and commentators did a sensible job of qualifying all the speculation with the proper observation that football was, at best, the most important of the unimportant things in life. The more the discussion and debate about the possibility of returning to any form of competitive football unfolded, the more obviously complex it became. Nonetheless, the return of top-level football installed itself with increasing force as some sort of signal that a kind of normality was achievable.

As the pandemic swamped all aspects of public and private lives, the UK government did its level best to deflect attention from international comparisons. As the numbers grew inexorably higher than those in Spain and Italy, the daily press briefing from Downing Street became an increasingly squirmy affair for whichever poor sap had drawn that day's short straw. In footballing terms, France and Holland had already given up the ghost, as had Scotland, notwithstanding a hilariously inept legal challenge from aggrieved Rangers. Belarus provided the only startling exception to this footballing blackout. Its leagues continued, encouraged, no doubt, by the Trump-like pig-ignorant view of its leader, Alexander Lukashenko, that no one was going to die of coronavirus in Belarus unless they were old or obese. There were 20,000 cases and 116 deaths by the start of May. Crowds flocked to the games in their dozens.

The four biggest European leagues – those in England, Germany, Spain and Italy – expressed a determination to see matters completed for the season. Germany's thorough and systematic testing arrangements meant that infection and death rates remained significantly lower than those in the UK. On 7 May, Chancellor Merkel announced that the Bundesliga would resume a week later. Whether this had any effect on the actions of the UK government can only be a matter for conjecture, but at around the same time, ministers again decided it was time to start talking about football.

Foreign Secretary, Dominic Raab, the man who had found himself pallidly clinging on to the podium during Boris Johnson's illness, expressed the view that the return of the Premier League would 'lift the spirits of the nation'. Now Raab is a karate black belt, so he understands sporting endeavour and he's probably not a man with whom to find yourself in a personal tangle. All the same, this must have sounded a bit rich (if you'll pardon the pun) to the players. One week you're the greedy scoundrels pinching an inflated wage when the rest of the nation is struggling to make ends meet; the next, you're the guardians of the country's morale. Let's be generous to Raab and his colleagues and not ask exactly how your morale will be lifted if the completion of these games ended in disaster for the team you support. Football, in all its importance, was almost certainly coming back to public life.

In mid-May the Bundesliga resumed. Just in case we all thought those clear-headed Germans had it all sussed, there were some hilariously strange contradictions in how the games were set up. Unsurprisingly, as soon as competitive instinct took over, full physical contact resumed as normal. Players pushed, shoved and jostled and breathed down each other's necks. Meanwhile, in the stands, substitutes sat at least two metres from each other in masks which were duly removed the moment they entered the field of play. Players bumped elbows or fists in celebration but forgot not to give each other a quick hug at the final whistle. On our sofas and chat groups we toyed, half-heartedly, with the idea of adopting a team to support. A careful scouring of the web reveals no indication as to whether this odd spectacle – enhanced by the use of cardboard cut-out crowds in some instances – did anything to raise German national morale.

What it did do was go a long way to honouring the contract between the league and the broadcasters. One can only imagine the urgency that this injected into various virtual boardrooms throughout the UK, but by the end of May, Project Restart became an entity – at least in the minds of the paymasters at Sky and BT. Tests for Covid-19, so difficult to locate and carry out, even for some of the most important key workers, became available for players and staff. Awkward individuals like Troy Deeney, who wanted to remind us that BAME players were at significant statistical risk and that not all players lived in glorious isolation in remote mansions, were given airtime, but their concerns were brushed aside. In a reflection of a national narrative that privileged the need to return to comfortable familiarity rather than confront infection and death rates that remained stubbornly high, the Premier League scheduled its return for the middle of June.

On the evening of Wednesday, 17 June, exactly 100 days after the whistle blew on Leicester and the Villa at the King Power Stadium, the Premier League returned to TV screens. In a delicious twist of fate, it had been a footballer who had dominated the front-page headlines for the previous two days. Marcus Rashford had conducted his own high-profile campaign to dissuade the government from scrapping free school-meal vouchers during the summer holidays. With all the foresight and firmness of purpose it had exhibited in the previous three months, the government almost immediately effected a welcome change of policy. And as if to prove that the whirligig of time really does bring in its revenges, Health Secretary Matt Hancock – he who had led the charge for these spoilt brats of players to take a pay cut – promptly forgot Rashford's name when being questioned about what the player's actions had achieved.

By the time the top clubs, followed shortly after by those in the Championship, took to the field, those in the lower divisions had had their fates all but tidied up. With no TV income to offset expenses, most of these clubs were faced with staging games – and thus incurring expenditure on wages and other resources – at what had to be a financial loss. A points-per-game calculation granted promotion to those in the automatic places and relegation for those similarly placed. Play-offs remained for those still in with a chance of climbing a division.

On the very evening of the restart, Barrow had their promotion from the National League confirmed. Six other clubs, with some significant Football League pedigree among them – Halifax, Barnet, Notts County, Yeovil, Harrogate and Boreham Wood – would contest a convoluted play-off arrangement, staged at their own cost and incurring a further £100,000 between them to carry out the necessary testing for the virus. Things were beginning to take some sort of shape. On the field of play, in an attempt, perhaps, to effect some kind of symmetry with the flaky goalkeeping of the last game before lockdown, Villa keeper Ørjan Nyland pretty well carried the ball into the Holte End only to be reprieved by a cataclysmic failure of both goal-line technology and the application of VAR. Welcome back to football.

What follows in this book is an attempt to capture something of what football was like during this strange, other-worldly period. If ever a word has been done to death since March, it is 'unprecedented' – but there is no disputing its aptness. The chapters that follow present a contemporaneous account of what happened to a range of clubs as football stumbled back to life. The choice of clubs is almost, but not entirely, random. There is an attempt to get a view across a range of settings and to give voice to a range of opinions. However, final choices were made for me, particularly at the higher level, by the willingness of those connected with the dozens of clubs I approached to respond to my initial approaches, made in early May 2020.

There was always going to be a problem. As no one's ever said on *Mastermind*, 'I've started, but I've no idea how I'll finish.' My intention was to paint a picture of clubs and supporters and assess how they were gearing up to the season that was about to finish in splendid TV or streamed isolation. I wanted to track and trace, if you'll pardon the expression, their progress as they approached the new season. You'll have spotted an immediate flaw: precisely when that new season was going to start and under what circumstances was a mixture of hope and guesswork. I make no apology if that uncertainty hovers over much of what follows, but I do hope that what emerges is as clear and as honest an account of what our relationship with football looked and felt like in those troubled months from March 2020.

Chapter 2

The Premier League. Burnley. Up with the big boys and surviving with ease

In the 2019/20 season, the TV money from broadcasting football was worth £8.65 billion to football clubs in England. Ninety-three per cent of that cash went to clubs in the Premier League and most of it went directly to players in wages. Football supporters, some steeped in the history and tradition of their unglamorous teams, and those whose affiliations with the giants runs deeper than fashion or glory-hunting, have always seen the unfairness of this imbalance. A fraction of the money sloshing around could be deployed to keep some smaller clubs afloat: the demise of Bury and the plight of Bolton at the start of the season brought this into sharp relief. The 'solidarity' payments made by Premier League clubs have done little to address this unevenness and while many who follow the game can happily gawp at unattainable talent and ability, there is a clear understanding that the rewards gleaned by the mega-rich won't be dribbling down to them any time soon. The upheaval of Covid might yet bring about some rethinking about redistribution.

Among other stadia built to woo affluent, middle-class newcomers, refreshingly lacking a flouncy, thin-skinned manager and almost devoid of Mediterranean thoroughbreds of any sort, stands Burnley. Away supporters can enjoy a hospitable pre-match pint at Burnley Cricket Club, the home of England legend (and that's not a lazy cliché) Jimmy Anderson, and a short stroll takes you to Turf Moor with its capacity of just under 22,000.

And here's something worth taking in: should the ground be full, that would represent nearly a quarter of the town's population. As with many clubs situated in areas with a significant number of people with Asian heritage, brown faces are few and far between – something of which the club is conscious and has made steps to address in its academy recruitment and other outreach activities. But the startling bottom line is this: surrounded by a choice of top clubs, with its income limited by a small ground and a general ambience that could never be deemed glitzy, Burnley survives in the top division with a degree of comfort. When Covid struck, they sat cosily in tenth place with 39 points from 29 games.

They were once the best team in the land – and they were once very nearly the worst, at least in terms of the fully professional game.

In 1960 they won the First Division title, squeezing past swanky Tottenham and Wolves on the last day of the season. They were managed by Harry Potts – and there's the sort of name you don't hear too often nowadays – and were presided over by chairman Bob Lord. Much has been written about Lord, which is unsurprising. Propelled by great energy and enthusiasm, he appeared to be guided by nothing more than an unremitting confidence in the rectitude of his own opinions and his individual wisdom, all of which were underpinned by egotism of skyscraper proportions. It would have been worth buying tickets to have seen him front up against some of his sleeker counterparts in the modern era.

1960 wasn't Burnley's first title; they had won the league in 1921 and although it did turn out to be their last, in 1962 they fetched up in second place behind the embodiment of total football that was Ipswich Town. Thirty-six years later things looked rather different. On the final day of the 1997/98 season, Burnley went into the last day needing a victory to assure their continued presence in the Football League. 18,811 people turned up to see them secure survival by beating Plymouth Argyle. At the other end of the table, Watford were champions. Bournemouth failed to make the play-offs but Fulham managed to do so, only to fall at the first hurdle against Grimsby Town. Wigan and Blackpool finished in mid-table anonymity, so that was five sides in the bottom tier who went on to enjoy their time in the starlight at various points over the next 20 years or so.

During that period, Burnley inched their way up the divisions, achieving promotion to the Premier League in 2009. There ensued half a dozen years of the sort of controlled yo-yoing that has worked well enough for themselves and West Brom, since when they have remained in the top division since 2016, with a brief, but somewhat scratchy, excursion into the half-world of Thursday night Europa League stuff. Their crowds remain firmly in the 20,000 region and their wage bill, as far as any sort of transparency allows a judgement to be made, reflects this. They are a solid, mid-table stalwart of the top division – at least for the time being – and that is why I chose them to provide a window into the process of football returning at the highest level. That, and the fact that their media team were unique in the Premier League in responding to my request for information – which also probably tells us something.

A spokesperson from that media team was pleased to tell me that the future of non-playing staff at the club remained secure. 'Some were furloughed during the lockdown period, and once the season starts some will continue to be, but the club anticipates re-employment once we get back to a normal situation.' The club, he went on to tell me, had been able to maintain links with those whose work in the area and Burnley FC looked forward to 'slowly opening its doors again to the local community'.

By the end of May it was confirmed that Premier League fixtures would be fulfilled. A glance at the online version of the *Burnley Express* – news you can trust since 1877 – revealed it to be in the same boat as all media great and small when it came to offering certainty to its readers. As far as was known, Burnley would play their first game late in June away at Manchester City. The *Express* made a valiant attempt to squeeze news out of the return to training of Jay Rodriguez and the usual daft old guff about 'transfer targets' which fluffs up so many dull column inches. If its readers were awaiting any great insight from the usually forthright lips of manager Sean Dyche, they would have been disappointed. Dyche could offer little other than the usual platitudes about getting players in good shape, keeping everyone safe, the oddity of playing behind closed doors and being happy to get back to some sort of normality. Fair enough – he knew as little or as much as anyone else.

For a bit of local colour, the story of the plight of Dave Burnley took some beating. Having changed his name by deed poll in 1976, Dave last missed a match in 1969 – Ipswich away. Lost 2-0, since you'll certainly want to know. Dave doesn't drive but walks, bikes, uses public transport and gets himself into all sorts of worldwide scrapes to watch the Clarets. His appearance in the *Express* stemmed from his revelation that he had a cunning plan to somehow inveigle himself into the locked-out games and thereby maintain this glorious record. No doubt the intrepid investigative journos attempted to track, trace and report on his progress. To be fair to Dave, he has not been deterred from going to games, including internationals, by war, industrial action, disease or pestilence, so there was no doubting the firmness of his resolve. The *Express* didn't say if he had a girlfriend.

On the fans' forum, discussion about the return of football was largely well-informed and thoughtful. In a move that I saw replicated by other clubs on independent platforms, *Up the Clarets!* had broken with the usual practice of separating formerly excluded political conversation from the main board during the pandemic. So, even though the post dealing with football's return had elicited some 630 responses a couple of days into

June, it was one headed simply 'Donald Trump' which had prompted around 800 more. Both topics faded into insignificance in comparison to the ongoing examination of the entrails of Brexit at 22,000 plus – over 10,000 more than a general thread about Covid-19. I'm not sure what, if anything, this tells us about the mindset during lockdown of your average Burnley fan – or any other supporter, come to that. What was clear from the interchanges was that, in something of a direct contrast to the daily obfuscation and ridiculous cheerleading coming from the political class, there was an appreciation that at least football was cobbling together something of a genuine plan. Amazing what the possibility of legal action to reclaim broadcasters' fees can do.

The chat online was enlivened by naysayers of various sorts – behind closed doors is rubbish; why not use this or that arithmetical formula?; is football really that important? – but if a consensus did emerge it was generally supportive of, if cautious about, the restart. Had I been looking at either of the other two sides in the Premier League in claret and blue – West Ham and the Villa, both in danger of relegation – I doubt that the overall feeling would have been quite as relaxed. Burnley's official website, however, was the epitome of the bland, formulaic layout and content so typical of their sort. No controversy here: the gaffer is raring to go; we're optimistic about Jay's fitness; we've got our eye on some great potential signings …

By the time Burnley resumed their season on the evening of Monday, 22 June, everyone else in the division had played at least once. As sofa-bound spectators, we had learnt a thing or two. First, the sound of an echoey stadium was infinitely preferable to the 'soundtrack' option being offered by most broadcasters – although I'll concede that this wasn't a unanimous point of view. Second, these early matches revealed that players were obviously not at peak fitness and, as a consequence, games were punctuated with errors that sometimes bordered on the elementary. For those of us whose playing days were enacted on the bobble and scratch of parks' pitches and whose performance, just occasionally, may have been inhibited by diets and alcoholic intake that were less than optimal, there was something rather comforting about this. But maybe most tellingly, teams seemed unable to find the extra spurt, push or boost of energy that a crowd may have provided.

The news that Burnley would be going into their opening game disadvantaged by injuries to three key players temporarily held sway on the fans' forum over Brexit, Trump and Covid. With the club already in the process of releasing players – in common with many others away from the very top of the tree – the discussion thread moved quickly away from the playing perspective to overall planning and financial management. In a reflection of a growing discourse about post-Covid football, many contributors expressed concern about a seemingly worrisome wage bill. Others uttered the unthinkable: maybe Dyche, SD, would be tempted elsewhere in the face of this uncertainty. And one sole poster – and those of us burdened with serial pessimism as protection against our clubs' enduring incompetence will relate to this – pointed out that far from looking at a place in Europe, one point was probably still required to ensure survival in the Premier League. Against this background, Burnley went into their first post-lockdown game against ritzy Man City, who had already seen off a lame and disorganised Arsenal the previous week, and were duly given a proper hiding, 5-0.

That evening, *Up the Clarets!* was ablaze with incandescent fury and frustration. Almost none of it was directed at the weakened Burnley squad that did well to keep the superstars down to a mere five goals. The target for posters' wrath was whoever was responsible for flying a plane over the Etihad Stadium moments after kick-off and with the game itself barely under way. The slogan trailing the aircraft read 'White Lives Matter Burnley'. Before the discussion thread wandered off into the vortex of whataboutery, it was probably best captured by Rileybob's comment that 'this makes me ashamed and embarrassed to support Burnley, something I've hardly felt in 30 years'.

The head-shaking despair from those on the forum was mirrored with exemplary speed by those who formally represented the club and its fans. Before half-time the official website carried an unequivocal message dissociating itself from the stunt and unreservedly condemning the perpetrators. As the game finished, captain Ben Mee immediately insisted on being interviewed by TV.

> *It does not represent what we're about, the club's about, the players are about and what the majority of fans are about, I'm sure. It's a small minority of people and I'm really upset that happened. I'm ashamed and upset it's associated with our club – my club – and it's not something we want to see at all in the game. We totally condemn it and are embarrassed by it.*

In the days that followed, it emerged that the organiser of the deed was local boy, Jake Hepple. With wearisome predictability, he insisted that he had plenty of black friends, was not a racist and that 'we were not trying to offend the [Black Lives Matter] movement or black people'. This seemed a little at odds with images on his social media feeds, one of which saw him in fraternal embrace with the one-time leader of the English Defence League, Stephen Yaxley-Lennon, who calls himself Tommy Robinson after a notorious football hooligan. Lancashire Police decided that no criminal act had occurred but Hepple lost his job and his girlfriend was suspended from hers for posting racially offensive material. The club determinedly maintained high-profile anti-racist messages on its website from that point until the end of the season.

If football-related weeping and wailing on the forums was to be expected after the Man City defeat, it was in relatively short supply and what little of it there was soon faded into the air. With a genuinely depleted squad and the high-profile departure of former England goalkeeper Joe Hart keeping the media busy about the club and its wage bill, two consecutive 1-0 victories over Palace and Watford saw the club into eighth place in the division – vying for top place in the second tranche and with the distinct possibility of European football in the coming season, whatever and whenever that might turn out to be.

Tony Scholes sits on the committee of the Burnley Supporters' Club, along with his colleague, Barrie Oliver. I ask them both the same question and get pretty well the same answer. What about going into Europe again? Would you fancy it? In theory, they tell me, a good thing. In practice, with the strong possibility that games would be behind closed doors, the appeal fades.

Tony first went to Turf Moor in 1961, the year after Burnley were champions – 'impeccable timing' – and, as a consequence, about to play in the European Cup. Just as a quick historical footnote, this was a knockout cup competition between teams who were the champions of their country. Instituted in 1955, it was won on the first five occasions by Real Madrid, who were holders when Burnley entered the competition. Their last victory before this, 7-3 against Eintracht Frankfurt, was played out in front of 127,621 spectators at Glasgow's Hampden Park. To give an indication of the sparse nature of the competition in comparison with its bloated, modern counterpart, a bye in the preliminary round for Burnley took them to the last 16 to play Stade Reims of France, a club that had already established some pedigree in this competition. Like so many of the fancy-dan Euro-types, they couldn't hack it on a wet Tuesday in the north and Burnley were through to the quarter-finals, 4-3 on aggregate.

On 18 January 1961, nine-year-old Tony watched as his hometown team beat Hamburg 3-1. There is easily accessible footage of the game online and even through the grey and grime of the oddly angled footage, any football supporter will know that this is what we live for. In the end, the glorious night counted for nothing as Hamburg won the return, 4-1. The victory, in its turn, did them no good as they lost to the eventual runners-up, Barcelona (who had already disposed of the mighty

Real), who succumbed to Benfica in the final in front of a measly 26,732 people in Bern, Switzerland.

In the mid-60s the club had forays into the Fairs and UEFA Cups but it is obvious that for Tony, it was that first taste of continental spice that lingered. 'To be honest, after all the dreadful times that followed, and with us nearly going out of the league, I never thought we'd come anywhere close to playing in Europe again,' he tells me. In 2018, however, courtesy of an exceptional seventh-place finish, Burnley fans could start looking at the flights and ferries that would take them on those magical continental away days of sparklingly different beer, the delicacies of local cuisine and the occasional cultural foray of a stroll round the Old Town before the game. Or, as Tony succinctly puts it: 'I wait nearly 60 years to have a chance to see my team play away in Europe, and we end up with a bloody Scottish team.' Aberdeen. The Granite City. 232 miles away. There and back in a day if you put your foot down. The glamour that is the Europa League on a Thursday night.

As it happens, Burnley overcome their Scottish opponents and then, in turn, İstanbul Başakşehir. Tony is unable to join the few hundred of the Burnley faithful who swell the 4,503 in Turkey but is present when they win the home leg with a goal in extra time. And now, he tells me, we get 'a proper football club in a proper stadium' – Olympiacos in Athens. And after a good deal of toing and froing with travel companies ready to make a quick killing from Burnley's success, Tony is ready to make his way out there in late August 2018.

He tells me of arrangements that dictate that he and his fellow Burnley fans are shielded in the bubble of shuttle buses that take them to the ground which he admits, admiringly, 'is proper hostile', notwithstanding the hospitality that they had enjoyed in parts of the city beforehand. As for the game, a 3-1 defeat, Tony, in keeping with the compulsory tradition of all one-eyed fans, is entirely clear that 'we were done by the ref'. Which would all be standard fare were it not for the fact that the fount of all knowledge, Wikipedia, remarks rather blandly that 'Olympiacos owner Evangelos Marinakis [he who, allegedly, had brought Covid to Arteta and Arsenal] had reportedly entered the referee's room at half-time to vent his frustration at his performance.' A 1-1 draw at home was enough to ensure that Burnley's brief incursion into sunshine and sangria was to terminate before the end of August, by which time they had failed to win in the league. Whether as a result of their adventure or not, the first half of their season was a disaster and they were second from bottom at Christmas. A terrific run of form thereafter saw them finish in a relatively comfortable 15th, but the question lingers: was the European diversion worth it – and would it be so now in this new world?

The club spokesperson tells me rather blandly that 'resources would be stretched, but the club would welcome European football for the second time in four years'. Tony and Barrie are as one in echoing this view. We don't think we're ready for it with such a thin squad; it may muck up the forthcoming season – whatever that may look like – it'd be pretty rotten behind closed doors … but, but, but – there may still be a bit of magic to be gleaned from it all. And there we have it. The reason that football is, indeed, important. Grown adults, sensible people with jobs, obligations, families and allotments. People who live through genuine trials and tribulations, both private and, in the months from March 2020, very public, cling to a dream and a shared hope of glory that will be transient at best and largely unnoticed by the world at large. If we'd beaten Olympiacos, we'd have been in a group with AC Milan. Just imagine. Yep – imagine. That's what we do.

As it happens, matters gradually slipped out of Burnley's hands. Five points in the three games after the Palace victory, including one gained by being the first side not to lose at Anfield in the league all season, would normally have been a creditable return. However, as clubs around them began to pick up points, any lingering hope of sneaking into a European place was punctured by a summary report of the proceedings of the Court of Arbitration for Sport (CAS) on 13 July.

The CAS overruled UEFA's verdict that Manchester City owner Sheikh Mansour bin Zayed al-Nahyan had disguised millions of his own funding as independent sponsorships from companies in Abu Dhabi. As a result, the potential two-year ban on City playing in European competitions was lifted. In a peculiar and alarming twist, the CAS also ruled that the club had not only failed to cooperate with the investigations of European football's governing body but had actually obstructed its investigations. For this, City were fined €10 million, almost certainly necessitating some ferreting down the back of a palatial sofa to locate the small change required for an organisation with revenues of £535 million in the previous year. For Burnley, it meant that only seventh place in the table would give them a chance of some continental action.

On the *Burnley Banter* Facebook page, the response to such a possibility wasn't even lukewarm. 'We don't want that again,' wrote a worried Andrew Taylor, 'we can't even fill a bench.' Jack Dean agreed, suggesting that what was needed were 'two teams for Europe campaign, which leads directly into the following season … and … almost cost us Premier League place. Players didn't get a proper rest.' Colin Walker couldn't see what fun it would be anyway. 'If fans are allowed to travel to Europe,' he pointed out, 'do you realise how expensive this is – travelling in Europe is far more expensive than the USA – lol.' Any enthusiastic voices were notable only for their silence.

In the end, it was all immaterial. Four points from the final three games after holding off Liverpool resulted in Burnley, with a creditable 15 points from their nine games in lockdown, finishing in the same tenth place they had occupied beforehand. In this, they shared the same outcome as half of the clubs in the division. Sean Dyche expressed justifiable satisfaction with what had been achieved. 'It's been quite interesting,' he told the club's website, going on to recognise the challenges faced in getting the show back on the road: 'I'm sure some have found it harder and more confusing, but we feel our work has gone well and been rewarded.'

Over on *Up the Clarets!*, although his achievements were given due recognition by most, the possibility of his move elsewhere elicited strangely tainted praise. Top Claret suggested that 'Dyche has done an amazing job for us but still has things to prove.' Meanwhile, the official spokesperson told me how 'the return of supporters is going to be crucial' in the coming season where revenue from broadcasting rights remained critical. Overall, though, there was no doubting the feeling that the post-lockdown venture had been a job well done. Dave Burnley, probably poring over cycle routes and amended train timetables in preparation for a new season, was unavailable for comment, while in a bitter twist, Burnley and the East Lancashire region found themselves the victims of a tightening of restrictions just as the revived season came to an end. It turned out not to be the last of the local lockdowns as the virus reminded us all too regularly that, football returning or not, it was still with us.

How lockdown changed the Premier League (not much, as it happens). Norwich should have stayed in their pyjamas and Villa pull off an unlikely escape.

Final position		Games post–lockdown	Points gained	Change post–lockdown
1.	Liverpool	9	17	-
2.	Man City	10	24	-
3.	Man United	9	21	+2
4.	Chelsea	9	18	-
5.	Leicester	9	9	-2
6.	Tottenham	9	18	+2
7.	Wolves	9	16	-1
8.	Arsenal	10	16	+1
9.	Sheffield Utd	10	11	-2
10.	Burnley	9	15	-
11.	Southampton	9	18	+3
12.	Everton	9	12	-
13.	Newcastle	9	11	-
14.	Crystal Palace	9	4	-3
15.	Brighton	9	12	-
16.	West Ham	9	12	-
17.	Aston Villa	10	10	+2
18.	Bournemouth	9	7	-
19.	Watford	9	7	-2
20.	Norwich	9	0	-

Chapter 3

Something else – black lives – mattered

The daft stunt with the plane in Burnley was significant. It reminded us that although football could have convinced us that it might be marginally important, it remained pretty trivial in the greater scheme of things. And just in case the world as we knew it wasn't being already shaken to its foundations by Covid-19, a shock of equal, life-changing force was about to shudder across the globe.

On 25 May in Minneapolis, Minnesota, a white police officer, Derek Chauvin, arrested a 46-year-old black man, George Floyd. Floyd may have been trying to pass off a counterfeit bill. Chauvin, with the aid of a number of colleagues, handcuffed Floyd, forced him to the ground and then proceeded to kneel on his neck for nearly nine minutes. Despite his protestations that he couldn't breathe, as well as pleas from onlookers to release him from this deadly manoeuvre, Chauvin maintained this stranglehold, refused to release it even when medical assistance arrived and so presided over the corpse of his own making. The entire vile episode was captured on mobile-phone footage.

In the days that followed, protests rocked towns, cities and even isolated rural communities around the world. They weren't just about Floyd's murder. By the end of May, it had become startlingly clear that Covid-19 disproportionately affected people from black and ethnic minority backgrounds and that the roots of this disadvantage lay in social and economic circumstances. Poorer people living in crowded conditions, doing poorly paid jobs without adequate protection, forced to use public transport if they did have jobs to go to and unable to shield themselves from the worst of the virus, were more likely to be from non-white communities. When mealy-mouthed commentators and politicians tutted that their choice to take to the streets to protest was a public health issue, such objections were met with wry laughter: how much more danger do you think we could be in anyway?

Floyd's murder prompted the dreadful roll call of young black men killed when under arrest or in police custody, which struck a chord way beyond the USA. Whether it was the disturbing coincidence of George

Floyd's death with the uneven suffering of black people from the virus, or whether it was simply an 'enough is enough' moment – and, for what it's worth, I believe it to be both but with the former feeding into the latter – the events in Minneapolis opened up a discourse that had been hiding in dusty, academic and political corners for decades. Racism, structural racism, deep embedded racism supported by the institutions of states and their governments, remains a fact of life – even in those societies that fancy themselves liberal, open-minded and way past such bigotry. And football, far from being a colour-blind island, is not free from this stain.

On the pitch, significant numbers of people of colour play for teams at all levels. The main point at issue is hardly original but remains alarming: while those doing the playing are representative of people from all over the world, from a range of ethnic, religious and cultural backgrounds, those in the managers' offices remain resolutely white. Across all divisions of senior football in the UK, fewer than four per cent of all managers are of BAME or non-white origin. The League Managers Association reported in 2018 that two-thirds of those managers who did secure a post were unable to get a second job. And if you think it's bad when it comes to managers, don't even think of looking in boardrooms where non-white faces are even rarer.

Almost from nowhere, the notion of structural racism, so clearly understood for so long by its victims, became a clear and obvious evil that needed to be confronted. For once, football and footballers did not hide. Jadon Sancho, playing in the echoey silence in the Bundesliga, set the tone by revealing a message of support for Floyd after scoring for Borussia Dortmund. In the days that followed, groups of players throughout the UK paused during training to be photographed 'taking the knee', the gesture originated by NFL quarterback Colin Kaepernick and adopted by thousands during the Black Lives Matter protests. Rio Ferdinand ventured to one of the public protests, taking his wife and three children with him, explaining that 'educating the next generation is an absolute must. For our children to have been a part of such an important protest is something that I'm sure will have a lasting effect on them.' Ian Wright, increasingly unafraid to tackle issues of race and football, revealed some of the appalling abuse directed towards him on social media and talked of how he was 'tired' – a term frequently used by black people – of trying to explain to white people about what it was like to live with the constant nag and pain of daily racism. Sometimes its manifestations are snide or even unconscious; all too often they are crude and malicious.

One player among hundreds who will be horribly aware of blunt, naked racism is Raheem Sterling. At

25 years old, having already achieved major success in the game, Sterling has found himself a compelling, if possibly unlikely, advocate for addressing injustice in football. At the start of June, he appeared on the BBC *Newsnight* programme to talk about the protests and, in a more general way, racism in wider society. When asked by Emily Maitlis – herself a victim of the boneheaded BBC hierarchy for daring to suggest that the government's handling of the epidemic had been shambolic – whether he considered those on the street to be acting carelessly, Sterling's answer was striking in the clarity of its message and the calmness of its delivery: 'the only disease we're fighting right now is racism'. Did he think that by speaking out he was making his job harder? 'I don't think about my job. I think about what's right.'

Sterling may be the first to admit that he has turned out to be an improbable interviewee on a flagship news programme. His early life and his experience of the education system had not been easy; it is clear, however, that he is a young man for whom that experience has fostered a commitment to the needs of others. His donations to various charities are measured in significant six-figure sums, ranging from work with the African-Caribbean Leukaemia Trust to supporting the victims of the Grenfell Tower disaster. In April 2019 he paid for over 550 pupils from his old school to attend the FA Cup semi-final at Wembley. Like many of his fellow professionals, Sterling has used his position to raise large sums of money to combat the coronavirus outbreak. Such public spiritedness sits in glaring contrast to the picture painted of him largely, but by no means exclusively, by the right-wing press.

This ludicrous, racist onslaught reached its grim apogee just before the start of the 2018 World Cup when eagle-eyed photographers spotted a rather amateurish tattoo of a gun on his right leg. Sections of the tabloid press made the immediate and obvious conclusion. Black boy, Jamaican heritage, too much money, a bit daft – obvious: he's glorifying gun violence and encouraging people to go out and shoot each other. No? Me neither. But when put together with a range of heinous misjudgements on his part, it was pretty obvious; we had a bad 'un on our hands. The list of his misdemeanours really is too long to include here – the doughty Adam Keyworth has compiled the absurdist list of shame on Twitter – but here's a flavour: he enjoyed an ice cream with his fiancée after England had just been beaten by Croatia; he bought his mum some nice new kitchen fittings, the show-off; talking of which, he showboated too much after scoring a hat-trick; he booked an £80 EasyJet flight, the cheapskate; and then he splashed out 50k on a new Merc, the flash git.

If there's possibly some grim humour in this litany of idiocy, it's still pretty hard to raise a smile.

The tabloid report which started by telling us that 'two more teenagers were killed over the weekend as Sterling revealed his controversial tattoo' plumbed a grubby vindictive depth, played out against tragic loss of life. In December 2018, shortly after having suffered clear racist abuse during a defeat at Chelsea, Sterling probably had an 'enough is enough' moment of his own. He tweeted: 'all I have to say is have a second thought about fair publicity and give all players an equal chance'. The incident that prompted his comment, after he'd endured the frothing insults of fat dads in replica kits who should know better, is illuminating.

Tosin Adarabioyo was a Manchester City player on loan to West Brom at the time. He bought his mum a house. Eighteen-year-old Phil Foden, who was enjoying occasional first-team appearances, did the same. Good boys. Adarabioyo's gift to his mother was captured in this headline: 'Young Manchester City footballer, 20, on £25,000 a week, splashed out on a mansion on market for £2.25 million despite having never started a Premier League match.' Foden's purchase was couched in language of a very different sort: 'Manchester City star Phil Foden buys new £2 million home for his mum.' In a perverse reversal of the idea of the deserving and undeserving poor, here we had the same for a pair of rich boys, one black, one white.

On the same night that Sterling appeared on *Newsnight*, Micah Richards had spoken on BBC Radio 5 about how he, and probably hundreds of black footballers, experienced the unsubtle hum of racist language and attitudes during his career:

> *I had just played for England, I was black, I had an Audi and a Range Rover. There were a couple of stories circulating about me and I got labelled the 'bling king'. But every week there was a story about me saying I wasn't concentrating on football and it took me six or seven years to shake that tag off. I remember my agent saying a team were interested in me but they weren't sure about your private life and I'm thinking 'hold on, you are judging me, you don't know me'. I knew that I had to change to fit in. I have a personality and I like to joke but for two years in training I was silent because I didn't want anyone to judge me on my character.*

As black players past and present – along with other black sportspeople, rock stars and others in the public eye – saw this as a moment in history to speak out, to maybe shake off the 'tiredness' and reserve that had inhibited them in the past, racism in football became a central part of the conversation as the game worked out how to face the post-Covid future. On the late afternoon of 17 June, as referee Michael Oliver blew the whistle to start the first game of the renewed season, players, coaches and ground staff at Villa Park, black and white, all took the knee. It was a scene that would have been unthinkable – and probably incomprehensible – two weeks before it occurred. A couple of hours later in the second game of the evening, the first goal of the restart was scored. By Raheem Sterling.

By necessity in the weeks that followed, football without crowds became the sole preserve of broadcasters. In terms of television, apart from a handful of games allocated to the BBC, much of this remained firmly sheltered behind various paywalls. If this had the potential of compromising the TV companies in terms of how they covered Black Lives Matter, their response was admirably unequivocal. Sky, for all of its political provenance in the Murdoch camp, badged its pundits and firmly placed the BLM logo on its backgrounds and settings. The company proudly announced that it was ensuring that all commentators were undertaking training in unconscious bias. Whether as a result of this or not, those same commentators made no attempt to glide over the importance of what was happening and even spoke with confidence about long-standing wrongs being addressed. Football, like the rest of society, had been unable to avoid the impact of Covid-19. When it came to Black Lives Matter, it showed a collective consciousness about racism that it had striven to evade for decades.

Not that this step towards any kind of progressive thinking met with universal approval – even though most of this criticism of the game's response came from people whose comments revealed that they probably wouldn't know a goal kick from a slam-dunk. Writing in *The Spectator* – the magazine in which Boris Johnson had once had to apologise for writing that Liverpool fans were habitual drunks and 'hooked on grief' – snarky gossip columnist Miss Steerpike seized on something written by Karl Henry. Karl, he of the kamikaze tackle and intemperate tweet, last turned out professionally for Bradford City in December 2018 – a good five years after he left Wolves. This had obviously passed Miss Steerpike by as she roundly praised 'the Wolverhampton captain' for pointing out that support for the idea of BLM is not the same as supporting the organisation. Miss S, as she likes to dub herself, has allies in her scepticism. For a collection of the crazed and deluded, they take some beating.

Writing on the Conservative Woman website under the headline 'Premier League kneels to BLM tyrants', Gary Oliver – conservative woman? – frets about players' numbers being replaced by the BLM slogan across their shoulders. How will we know who they are? *Spiked*, a self-styled 'voice of the people' in an age of destabilising political correctness, moans that it is 'bizarre that football ever became an arena for the culture war'. The Breibart website, founded by Dominic Cummings's role model and hero, Steve Bannon, claims that the Premier League, realising it had backed the wrong horse, was attempting to distance itself from BLM. It labelled the Premier League as a 'virtue signalling footballing establishment' before going on to cite a tweet supporting the benefits of free-market capitalism for black people from that most astute of observers and opponent of the BLM movement, Wolverhampton captain Karl Henry. In all of this strangeness, they were encouraged by a couple of unsurprising mainstream sources: *The Sun* and the *Daily Mail*.

For both papers, the wearing of the BLM badge by TV pundits became the theatre of war. As the movement evolved, mobilising increasing numbers of people following the death of George Floyd, those who had become engaged by its activities began to make connections with other global injustices, including global warming and Palestinian rights. For some pundits, this was a step too far and, it seems, they had asked their employers to be spared the obligation of wearing the badge. 'Sky Sports team ditch Black Lives Matter badges' *The Sun* proclaimed on 2 July before going on to concede that some of them were, in fact, wearing them.

Others were wearing Kick It Out ones instead. A few days later, the *Mail* took up the same theme: 'Just ONE pundit left wearing BLM badge.' And that pundit was Emile Heskey.

If Raheem Sterling has ever felt justifiably aggrieved by his treatment at the hands of the press and the public, Emile must know exactly how he feels. Excuse my using his forename in such familiar fashion: he once scored against the Villa and that cements our one-sided friendship forever. The title of Dean Eldredge's wonderful biography captures the view of plenty of supporters – usually of clubs for whom he had not played – in its faintly damning praise: *Even Heskey Scored*. Throughout all of this unwarranted criticism, it wasn't until he had finished playing that he, like many players, spoke about the enduring extent of racism in the game and of his experiences as a player.

> *If you got sour or upset about any of these things you generally wouldn't go anywhere in football. No black person controls anything within football so we had to fit in. It has to come out to let people understand what we had to go through and how tough we had to be to make it within football.*

The idea that black footballers had been through too much to ignore the importance of BLM to the game was given further force a few days after the jibe against Heskey in the *Mail*. If, for the ignorant, the idea persisted that Emile was some kind of throwback to the big-man-up-front centre-forward of a bygone era (and he was so much more than that), the same accusation could never have been levelled against sleek, streamlined Thierry Henry. On 10 July, in his capacity as manager of Montreal Impact, Henry took the knee for the full eight minutes and 46 seconds during which George Floyd was trapped beneath the knee of Derek Chauvin. In a contemporaneous comment on his Instagram account, with 2.6 million followers, he echoed much of what had already been said by black players, some of them for years: 'It's gone on for too long and we have come too far for this to be tolerated in modern society.'

Football's initial response to BLM had been to demonstrate that, for once, it was not going to circle the wagons and hide behind weary slogans of 'keeping politics out of sport'. As with so much that happened during lockdown, the way in which society organised itself found itself under daily scrutiny – not just by those who were charged with decision-making of the highest order, but by ordinary people going about their business and with a little more thinking space than usual. In common with many things that happened to us in that extraordinary spring and summer, we felt our way into an uncertain but, in this respect at least, an optimistic future.

Chapter 4

The Championship – where football remains at its stubborn best. Swansea get a miracle but don't quite make it

The Championship, the second division of English football, is a special animal – a dogged shire horse beside the pedigree dashers of the Premier League. By the time you've thrown in a few cup appearances, it's Tuesday and Saturday from the beginning of August until May starts to bloom.

You start off watching in shorts and tee shirt, progress to donning every layer of clothing you possess and finish up subject to the whims of an English spring, which can bring blazing sunshine and the last snowfalls – sometimes in the course of the same game. You will have picked up that this is familiar territory to me: I support Birmingham City.

For many people who carry the similar affliction of being hackled to a club whose motto should be 'We'll put you through the wringer and often let you down', getting through a Championship season as a supporter, never mind as a player, is usually a battle of endurance and duty. An episode a couple of years ago completely epitomised this for me.

Away at Reading on a Tuesday night in a steady autumnal drizzle. There are 14,602 people present, although it's impossible to believe that this official attendance isn't based on season-ticket numbers rather than turnstile clicks. As the teams emerge to tinny music and the puppyish enthusiasm of the stadium announcer, flags are unfurled and a fanfare blurts out. If this is meant to summon up the blood and stiffen the sinews of the, probably, 10,000 or so hardy souls who have trekked across retail parks trying to digest their tea, there's no obvious evidence of it having done so. We're here because we have no choice. It finishes 0-0. As the old cliché goes, both sides are lucky to get nil. Slumped and gawping in the comfort of their homes, the good citizens of Berkshire, and the thousand or so of us trying to keep awake in the away end, could be watching Arsenal play PSG or Celtic getting eviscerated by Barcelona. But, of course, we aren't. For all its workaday toil, football below the Premier League is still stitched firmly into the fabric of the game.

The number of people watching live Championship football is exceeded in Europe only by the Premier League and the Bundesliga. Eleven million people attended games in the last completed season. In the two divisions below, the total was seven million, with a staggering 15.5 million in the plethora of leagues below the fourth tier. When Covid-19 brought an end to football, the ongoing conversation about what the game would look like at all levels became a matter of thoughtful speculation. Up there at the top, the massive investment in terms of broadcasting rights, players' wages and, yes, the place of the game in the national psyche meant that nobody was going to start thinking about wringing the neck of this particular golden goose. What might happen below, at the level where the links between clubs and their supporters are entrenched in localities and strong traditions of family loyalty and history, would be played out in ways that were hazy at best.

The governing body of the 71 (since the demise of Bury) clubs that live outside the Premier League is the English Football League – the EFL. Readers can relax: it is not the main intention of this single volume to document the litany of odd decisions and edicts of this body and, besides, I've already let the cat out of the bag about my affiliations, thereby revealing that any such comment will be a touch jaundiced. Having said which, the EFL was left in a situation where the chance of achieving the greatest good for the greatest number might have been beyond its capabilities – and, on this occasion, through no fault of its own. Issues around promotion, relegation and play-offs were weighty and represented the absolute basis for existence for most clubs. And for many such clubs, staging games to complete the season, as desirable as that may have been, would entail expenditure that would probably not be offset by broadcasting income.

At the end of May, the EFL wrote to Championship clubs proposing that the season resume on 20 June. Although it appeared that most clubs had already begun to prepare for a restart at some point, the manner and timing of the EFL's suggestion was not met with universal approval. The most vocal of its critics was QPR's chief executive Lee Hoos, who complained about the short notice of the announcement and that 'there was an appalling lack of corporate governance. It dropped out of nowhere and that's what my real issue is: the process of how this was done. The clubs need to have a talk and come to a kind of consensus of how we take this forward.' Barnsley wrote to the EFL to express concern that any meddling with the format of games – extra substitutions, change to play-off qualification – meant that the season would 'be completed with a lack of sporting integrity'. Others tended to be more sanguine with a principal concern emerging about the time required to get players match fit. As with everything concerning football at the time – and in a reflection of what was going on in wider society – certainty about anything was at a premium.

In mid-March, the Championship table looked neat and tidy with all teams having played 37 games. West Brom and Leeds seemed to be strongly placed in the two automatic promotion places, although history, as well as Leeds's comical capacity to fall apart again, indicated that nothing was a foregone conclusion. A further truism about the Championship is that two consecutive wins can alter a team's position in the table dramatically and so Swansea City, in 11th place with 53 points, just three points short of the play-off places, could allow themselves to cling on to the notion that their season was far from complete. And just in case we were running out of platitudes about football in this division, it really is the case that anyone can beat anyone on a given day. This plays out in the congested points tally that squashes so many teams together and which also means that looking at future fixtures and trying to predict outcomes is complete folly. Precedent suggested that Swansea would, at the very least, need to win seven of their nine remaining games, so a couple of early failures offered the grim prospect of playing a series of meaningless games behind closed doors, with only a few of those games having any bearing on the key outcomes of promotion and relegation.

A visit to the official club website in the first week of June was a journey to the land of utter blandness. This rude observation is not one that is confined to Swansea: the official online presence of practically every club reveals little that has not already been pored over on social and mainstream media for days. The insipid fare of the website, mirrored with equal inanity in ridiculously overpriced matchday programmes, offers little genuine insight and, with the occasional honourable exception, evades controversy or disputatiousness at every turn. During Covid, most sites flopped out a meagre menu of great games from the past, reminiscences from such former stars as could be dragged up and, naturally, unmissable offers from the club shop. The generic message about the return to football from the EFL was badged with the Swansea logo and if there were any controversy about the resumption, particularly in a part of the UK where infection was at its highest at that time, you wouldn't have encountered any inkling of this being the case.

Incidentally, just in case you thought I may have overlooked it, I am fully aware that Swansea is in Wales and not England, but they have played in the English Football League since 1921. As the pandemic developed, so did schisms in the approaches of the devolved governments in the UK, but with the absence of potential crowds, this had little impact on Swansea's dual affiliations.

A skim through the history of Swansea City – Swansea Town until 1969 – shows a team residing in the lower reaches of the Football League for most of its existence until the second decade of the 21st century. Some of that time was in the second tier but the record is littered with visits to the lower strata. In 1981, however, the Swans were promoted to the First Division for the first time in their history and spent most of that season looking like potential league winners. A drop in form towards the end of the season saw them slip to sixth which was still a truly exceptional achievement.

There ensued three decades of wild volatility, but with most of the momentum being in an unstoppable downward direction. Following their season of glory, Swansea were relegated in 1983 and then slipped through the net to the Third Division in 1984. In 1985 they scrabbled to avoid the drop to the Fourth Division but determinedly completed the job in 1986. From there, they began a dogged ascent, reaching the play-offs in the second tier in 1993, losing in the semi-final to West Brom. Far from using this as a springboard to further success, more relegations followed in 1996 and 2001 and at the end of the 2002/03 season, like Burnley five years earlier, their survival in the Football League came down to the final game of the season. A 4-2 win against Hull in front of a crowd of 9,585 at the old Vetch Field – more follows – did the job ... and eight years later, once again in an emulation of Burnley's achievements, they were in the Premier League where they stayed with relative comfort as well as winning the League Cup in 2013 ... until they were relegated in 2018.

The Vetch was everything that football supporters of a certain generation wanted. Surrounded by local housing with plenty of pubs dotted around, bearing its shabby ageing with some grace and capable, as only the stadia of the era before the Taylor Report could be, of generating jangling excitement, especially under lights, the Vetch could be an intimidating and moody venue for away supporters. A comment on a blog set up in its memory captures a sentiment familiar to many because of a romantic, but authentic, recollection of seeing 'your' ground for the first time: 'that slightly nervous feeling of walking up the small concrete slope on to the north bank seeing the Vetch in all her glory in the sunshine in August is something that will live with me for the rest of my life'. In 2005 the old stadium was superseded by the Liberty Stadium, used by Swansea along with Ospreys rugby union club, and built by the local authority at a cost of £27 million. After years of financial circus acts, familiar to so many followers of Football League clubs, a supporters' trust has now established a 21 per cent shareholding.

With a thunderstorm rumbling in the background, I talk to one of the trust's leading lights, Cath Dyer – 'same as the player, Nathan, but no relation' – who is also chairperson of the club's disabled supporters' association. She refers throughout our conversation to the club owners simply as 'the Americans' although there is no great rancour in her comments and she talks of a degree of cooperation between the two bodies. In a moment of great humour, she tells me of how the club and trust worked together to address possible ways of compensating season-ticket holders for the games they have been unable to attend. In a move similar to many clubs in the Championship, Swansea offered either a straight refund or, for those fortunate enough to be so generous, a 'do nothing' option meaning, in effect, a donation to the club. Other than that, patrons could avail themselves of the club's streaming service to watch all remaining games. The final option was a lucky dip. I am, of course, intrigued.

The lucky dip, Cath tells me, is by far the most popular choice. I suppose I'm hampered by an idea of a raggedy old tombola at the local fete and so am surprised to hear her tell me of the degree of largesse bestowed on the recipients. An acquaintance has come away with two goalkeeper's jerseys, home and away, as well as a pair of shorts, a jacket and a bath towel. She has heard tales of similar bounty being enjoyed by many others.

Somewhere, I can only imagine, the kit person and the stock controller of the club shop are sitting, rocking in a corner with their heads in their hands. For all of that, the lucky dip has been a great success.

By the time we speak, the Swans have played three games since the restart. A 3-0 win at Middlesbrough ensured that the dream of scraping into the final play-off place remained a possibility. And then Swansea did to their supporters what every Championship side does – and, believe me, I know of what I speak. Gifted a home game against bottom-of-the-table Luton, they lose 1-0. On the forum, Bryn Cartwright captured it all: 'Typical Swansea performance against a bottom club. Why do we do this over and over again? I'm in despair and in need of a stiff drink already. FFS.' It probably wouldn't have helped Bryn's mood at that juncture to point out that there was nothing remotely unique about his team's ability to let the chance of enhanced mediocrity slip through its grasp. And he might not have seen the funny side of thornabyswan's enquiry as to whether the cardboard cut-outs had left yet, either. A draw away at Millwall lightened the mood a little, but, in the meantime, the worst was beginning to happen. With wins against Leeds and Preston, Cardiff City overtook their kind-of neighbours and nestled into sixth place.

Cath hesitates tellingly when I drop the C-word. Then, with charming understatement, she tells me that she 'doesn't particularly like Cardiff' and that 'the last thing we want if we don't go up is for them to do so'. She hasn't given up hope completely and believes that manager Steve Cooper is trying to put together a promising young team. Hers isn't a view widely shared on the forums but the reality that post-Covid football without crowds and big wages may need to be founded on such young players is an increasingly prevalent point of view. As for the future, Cath belongs firmly to the school of happily waving the 'big boys goodbye if they want to go off and form some super league of their own'. I put to her the notion of regional leagues below the top level and am only marginally surprised to hear her pride about playing in the English league and her slightly damning view about the possibility of being the big fish in the pond of a Welsh one.

We finish our conversation with me thanking her and expressing regret at the fact that when Swansea come to St Andrew's in a few days' time, I won't be able to buy her a pint to show my gratitude. Because that, of course, is all part of the business of playing at home, isn't it? On average, 48 per cent of games are won at home in the English Championship. After three rounds of games post-lockdown, this trend was firmly bucked. Nine of the 36 were draws, 12 were home wins and 15 were won by the away team. As it transpires, it is an upward trend that continues when Cath's boys come to Birmingham on a wet, miserable Wednesday evening where, despite going a goal down after four minutes, they stroll to a comfortable 3-1 win. Coupled with Cardiff's defeat at home to Blackburn the previous evening, the result puts them one point behind them in seventh place, with a superior goal difference and four games to go. I'm glad I don't have to meet Cath, or anyone, after yet another dire performance from my own team (I indulge myself in a brief documentation of this in a later chapter), but for the Swans, the dream is still on. As a footnote to the home-win percentage, it had levelled out to around 40 per cent by the time the season closed.

As the tussle for sixth place contrived to keep a handful of sides interested, the view from the forums made entertaining reading. Old Jack refused to get overexcited. 'There are very few prem quality players if any in our squad,' he warned. 'We'd need a new team if we got there and who's gonna pay? The prem is all about how much money you've got to throw away.' Such gloominess is rebuffed by Pego Jack who asks, 'What's football all about if it isn't about going as high as you can as often as you can?' JB confronts the doomsters who fear weekly humiliation if they do make it by reminding them of Sheffield United's remarkable achievements: 'according to the experts, they were likely to beat Derby's low points record' but are now pressing for Europe. What unites them as they head towards two crucial final games is their visceral hatred of their South Wales rivals – who are referred to in a range of terms of varying vulgarity – and the heartfelt wish that if the Swans don't make it, Cardiff must not be there in their place.

On the last day of the Championship season, Swansea are one of three clubs in contention for the final place. The odds are not in their favour. First and foremost, to have any chance, they need to win their own game away at Reading – who have nothing to play for. They then need Forest to lose quite substantially at home to Stoke – who have nothing to play for. And then they need Cardiff to lose at home to Hull, who have everything to play for because they would need the same sort of planetary alignment as Swansea in order to avoid relegation. However, they are bottom of the table for a reason – their complete and enduring ineptitude. As far as the 'being on the beach' trope is concerned, the research has yet to be done to endow it with any validity, but on a personal level, last days and entire seasons have been undone by teams putting in admirable performances when they had no apparent incentive for doing so.

I speak to a member of Swansea's media team on the morning of the game. I'm grateful for his time as he is, naturally, preparing for a very big day for the club. Under normal circumstances, the publicans in Reading could have been preparing for a bumper night as supporters from across the Severn barrelled down the M4 to drink them dry. Now, like all of us, they'll be on the edges of sofas, checking scores from elsewhere as they go. In times gone by, they'd have been photographed in grounds with transistor radios glued to their ears.

Liberated, perhaps, by the fact that Swansea's chances are those of the outsider, the spokesman tells me that everyone is looking forward to it. It's not intended as an insult to say that there is nothing surprising in what I'm told: 'We have to focus entirely on our own result; we can't be thinking about anyone else; we know there's a lot riding on it, but we've just got to do what we have to do.' I wish him well; after all, I've not got a dog in this fight. I explain that the evening will probably be much more tense for me and he sympathises courteously.

And the event is jaw-dropping. At the Cardiff City Stadium, things go to plan for the home side. They are soon a goal up against Hull and it looks increasingly unlikely that they will be caught. If Swansea are to have a chance, they need to win handsomely and for Forest to implode. Swansea go a goal up at on-the-beach Reading just as Forest go one down at home to on-the-beach Stoke. However, when Reading, now down to ten men, equalise just before half-time, the game looks up. Even if the Swans win and Forest lose, there is a goal difference of five in favour of the latter. Then the world goes a touch bonkers.

In the final half hour of the season, Forest score a goal which would ensure their place in the play-offs and then somehow contrive to promptly concede two more to Stoke who have nothing to play for. They're 3-1 down, on 70 points with a goal difference of nine. Meanwhile, Swansea score twice more to go 3-1 up. They now have 70 points with a goal difference of eight. And then they score again in the 91st minute. Both on 70 points, both on a goal difference of nine, but here's the crunch. Over the season, Swansea have scored three more goals and if things stay the same, they squeeze into the play-offs. Forest, aware of their predicament, push for the goal that will prevent this and, in doing so, allow Stoke, all now attired in floral shirts, flip-flops and eyeing up the margaritas in the dugouts, to break and score again in the 96th minute. On Sky Sports News, Jeff Stelling goes purple with excitement. Goodness only knows what's happening in the Welsh valleys.

'It was all a little bit of a blur at the end, to be honest,' admits manager Steve Cooper in his Zoomed press conference. His appearance on the club's website reflects this – he looks happily drained, if a little disorientated. Over on the fans' forum there is a mixture of elation and surprise before the inevitable descent into sniping and some odd one-upmanship. 'Let's just go easy on one another eh?' suggests Brymill Jack. 'We got to the play-offs somehow. Let's enjoy it!'

And for a while, the side that came out of lockdown with just the faintest of hopes do just that. With the occasional exception. Before the first leg, caller Paul on Radio 5's *606* programme surprises the spikey Chris Sutton by saying that, much as he's proud of his side, he'd still rather not get to Wembley if it meant playing Cardiff – 'they're still crowing about 1927 [when they won the FA Cup], God knows what'd happen if they beat us in the final'. His overall caution (although not necessarily about Cardiff) is reflected on the fans' forum, but a 1-0 win in the home leg against Brentford keeps the dream alive. The victory is aided and abetted by a peculiar red card flourished by referee Keith Stroud (who, believe me, has form when it comes to odd decisions) for a challenge by Rico Henry. It is rescinded within 48 hours.

Three days later they go to Griffin Park for the last game to be played on that wonderful, pub-surrounded ground and within 15 minutes, they're pretty well out of it, with Brentford two up in the game and bossing the show. Swansea try to keep it neat and fluid, but a minute after half-time, Brentford score again and despite a Swans goal with just over ten minutes to go to keep it alive, the show's over. Although he doesn't know it yet, caller Paul from *606* can relax: the following evening Cardiff, despite their best efforts, fail to turn over the two-goal deficit from their first-leg game with Fulham and so the play-off final will be decided by two clubs from west London in a deserted Wembley, some eight miles from their homes.

After the game, Steve Cooper can be excused for trotting out meaningless phrases about it being painful and not doing the basics. On social media, despite some outlandish criticism of his tactics and some of the players, there is broad acceptance that they'd kind of overachieved and finally been done by a better side. 'Yup, everyone can hold their heads up,' suggests Hobo. 'They gave themselves a chance and couldn't really have done much more. Some lethal finishing from Brentford has been the difference, and they deserve it overall. On to next season.'

On to next season indeed. What it'd look like and when anyone would be back in the Liberty to see it was anyone's guess … but on to next season. The eternal hope. And that hope, among talk of second waves and localised lockdowns, might just be one of the reasons that football really is important.

The Championship.
As mad as ever. Luton and Barnsley pull off the great escape – and Wigan pay the price despite stunning form. Leeds do not fall apart again.
How teams performed after lockdown.

Final position		Games post-lockdown	Points gained	Change post-lockdown
1.	Leeds	9	22	-
2.	West Brom	9	13	-
3.	Brentford	9	21	+1
4.	Fulham	9	17	-1
5.	Cardiff	9	19	+4
6.	Swansea	9	17	+5
7.	Forest	9	10	-2
8.	Millwall	9	14	-
9.	Preston	9	10	-4
10.	Derby	9	13	+2
11.	Blackburn	9	10	-1
12.	Bristol City	9	8	-5
13.	QPR	9	5	-
14.	Reading	9	8	-
15.	Stoke	9	14	+2
16.	Sheff Weds	9	8	-1
17.	Middlesbrough	9	12	+2
18.	Huddersfield	9	9	-
19.	Luton	9	16	+4
20.	Birmingham	9	3	-4
21.	Barnsley	9	15	+3
22.	Charlton	9	9	-
23.	Wigan*	9	18	-3
24.	Hull	9	4	-3

* Wigan deducted 12 points during lockdown for going into administration.

Chapter 5

Things fall apart ... not Leeds this time, but a few others

... as the poet WB Yeats almost famously wrote. The accurately transcribed lines of the poem could be inscribed in the offices of plenty of football clubs around the country. 'Things fall apart, the centre cannot hold ... anarchy is loosed upon the world.' Now, I'll be the first to concede that such grand parlance is a touch over the top when it comes to mere football, but trying to keep up with the runaway train of financial solvency while achieving any degree of success usually does turn out to look pretty anarchic.

As June ended and we became dozily accustomed to the deadened fare of TV football, some stark realities of what the post-Covid world might look like came into sharper focus.

On the first day of July, Wigan Athletic, who
had dragged themselves from a position of relegation
favourites to mid-table safety in the Championship with
three consecutive victories, went into administration.
This happened four weeks after a Hong Kong-based
consortium acquired the club and assured it of its secure
future. With thanks to journalist David Conn, I'll
borrow this paragraph from his report of events from
The Guardian of that day:

> *The club stated on 4 June that under the EFL's
> owners' and directors' test, the league had
> approved the sale to NLF (Next Leader Fund)
> by the owner since November 2018, International
> Entertainment Corporation (IEC), a Hong
> Kong-based, Cayman Islands-registered company
> which owns a hotel and casino in the Philippines.*

Now, I've been to Wigan on a few occasions and I'm not
going to lie: it's not one of my favourite awaydays. I don't
want to engage in clichés either, but it *is* famous for pies
and we do have a favourite spot where we park up and
partake of the fare on offer and it is delicious. Getting
a pint is more of a challenge as the DW Stadium, as
befits its no-frills label, is another of those situated
on retail premises away from traditional back-street
boozers. Crowds are not huge and tend to rattle around

the standard kit-built ground and, by and large, it's also one of those places where my team does not often enjoy success. If you play there in winter, it's a long journey home in the dark when you've lost. But not as far as the Cayman Islands, or Hong Kong or the Philippines.

The tenuous connection between those who spot an entity as a business opportunity and those who identify a local football club as part of their identity and culture could not be starker. This mismatch was made even more apparent when looking at the comments of the administrators, Begbies Traynor, charged with steering the club through its difficulties. 'Our immediate objectives,' they explained on the fateful day, 'are to ensure the club completes all its fixtures this season and to find interested parties to save Wigan Athletic FC and the jobs of the people who work for the club.' It might be fair to observe that a mere four weeks ago, someone *had* been interested enough to purchase the club but obviously suffered from a spectacular attack of buyer's regret. The body charged with ensuring the league's affairs are conducted with fairness and efficiency, the EFL, had deemed this purchaser, albeit via silent consent, to be fit and proper. Such a situation leaves nothing more to be said other than the fact that in its 147-word statement on its website, the EFL confined its comment to how and when the club would be deducted its 12 points.

One more comment from the administrators merits attention. 'Obviously,' they explain, 'the suspension of the Championship due to Covid-19 has had a significant impact on the recent fortunes of the club.' Which begs the question, 'What do you mean by fortunes?' In the nine games prior to lockdown, the Latics had taken 18 points from nine games and beaten league leaders, West Brom, away from home. Once restrictions were lifted, just to hammer home the point made above, they won three on the bounce. Looked at one way, there's an argument that says that Covid-19 most definitely had an impact on the fortunes of the club and that as far as playing football was concerned, it was highly beneficial. Regrettably for the club and its supporters, it was not the enormous achievements of Paul Cook and his players that counted for anything from Hong Kong to the Caymans to the Philippines.

On the fans' forums, reactions were sad and predictable. Pies'r'us reposted a letter he had made public in which he had identified the chairman and major shareholder of IEC plc, Dr Choi Chiu Fai Stanley, as both vendor and purchaser of the club. Pies – if I can make so bold as to use his informal name – suggested that Stanley was using the club purely as part of his financial portfolio to support a range of activities, one of which was alleged to be participation in high-end poker competitions. Others, too, were certain that they saw it coming, but the overall tone was genuinely one of sorrow rather than anger. And this sadness was echoed in the platforms of other fans, particularly those in the Championship and, tellingly, on those of Wigan's local rivals. Lumico from Blackburn captured a widespread view by revealing that 'I think I'll refrain from laughing at their demise – this could be us at any moment.' Raefil from Preston suggested that 'folk need to wake up and get realistic about signing players. I'm more interested in seeing our club survive right now – it's something no club can take for granted.'

He's entirely correct. A report from the major accountancy firm, Deloitte, revealed that in the 2018/19 season, clubs in the Championship spent 107 per cent of their revenue on wages: £785 million coming in, £837 million going out. That's just on wages. So, before a blade of grass has been cut, a pot of paint purchased or the air-dryer in the washrooms replaced, the money's all accounted for. To make matters worse, this profligacy – which in most cases is incurred in the hope of promotion to the sunny uplands of the Premier League – has been happening with obstinate regularity, year on year. This 'close your eyes and hope' approach to financial prudence is kept afloat by three lifebelts: contributions from board members, profit from transfers and the acquisition of the holy grail of promotion. Any such success, in turn, provides the temporary security of the parachute payment which permits clubs to drop again in the hope that this partial guarantee of revenue will enable immediate elevation. For a telling view of what happens when this goes spectacularly wrong, watch the compelling documentary series *Sunderland 'Til I Die.*

Deloitte's view is that a 70 per cent wage cap would go some way to correcting this descent into the financial vortex. Quite how this could work out remains one of the great imponderables as football adjusts itself to the post-Covid world, but the omens are not auspicious. At the height of the outbreak, players at Leeds and Birmingham reportedly made some moves towards deferral and reduction of wages, but similar reports are difficult to locate – none of which is to belittle the significant individual contributions from players to their communities. Nonetheless, as the Professional Footballers' Association (PFA) diplomatically pointed out in April 2020, it would have been unwise for players to hobble themselves to blind arrangements. In a letter to its members, the PFA announced its intention 'to see each club's financial situation before we offer advice to players on whether to accept the terms offered'. One can only imagine that it's going to be a busy year for that organisation and its officials. Without wishing to be snarky, it's difficult for me to gauge. Every attempt to communicate with them while writing this book was met with complete silence until, when pushed into response by my persistence, they eventually confirmed that they would offer no comment about anything.

As for what the shape of the future leagues might look like, once again the figures tell the story. In the pre-lockdown Championship, 24 teams made 21 per cent of their income from matchday revenue. As of July 2020, the possibility of that revenue being generated for at least a year was remote at best. Fifty-four per cent of revenue in the division is generated by TV. We have yet to see how popular a 'product' this will be in the strange new world of echoey, atmosphere-free stadia. In the light of these blocked streams of income, those fans who suppressed their sniggers at Wigan's ill fortune were right to do so. As the senior manager in the Sports Business Group at Deloitte put it:

> *While revenue-generation is a new problem for professional football, clubs have had a cost control problem for decades. The demise of Bury and the dangerous predicament many other Football League clubs find themselves in must move the game to introduce meaningful regulatory change and improvement.*

Earlier in the same week of Wigan's misfortunes, another footballing story of lost jobs, hopes and ambitions slipped under the radar a little. In some ways this was unsurprising as the sludge of bad news about potential redundancies in a range of industries slid down the hillside towards us. From shirt makers to sandwich cutters to aircrew, people whose livelihoods depended on other people going out of their houses for work or play saw their way of making a living under terrible threat. In the wake of a potential £300 million deficit in relation to the virus, the Football Association announced its intention to cut 124 jobs from its payroll. The chairman, Greg Clarke, presented a gloomy prognosis:

> *We don't know what the future holds. Having to put forward proposals that will reduce our headcount in order to solve our pressing financial problems is the most difficult decision the board and the senior management team has to make. The problem is that the pandemic will be followed by an economic recession. There will be problems that will last for years, so we must deal with them. But we must deal with them with compassion for our people and respect for the team. All areas of the FA will be affected.*

There was a grim irony about both Clarke's comments and the day on which he made them. For many football supporters, the FA – which, to be fair, does its level best to try to make a meaningful contribution to grassroots football – is synonymous with Wembley Stadium. Argument rages about its use for football and while the one thing on which the majority of supporters seem to agree is that employing it for the semi-finals of the FA Cup tarnishes the achievement of getting to Wemberlee for the final, the democratisation of its use for other trophies and play-off finals is generally welcomed. Of the 91 teams in the top four divisions in 2019/20, only Crawley Town and Accrington Stanley have never made an appearance there, either before or after its renovation. The arch has improved the rather stark aesthetics of the twin towers, but parking remains a nightmare, although the revamped Wembley Park tube is a huge improvement on its predecessor. Food, drink and match programmes are absurdly dear. Yet for all of these irritants, going to Wembley to watch your team – once the stuff of impossible dreams for the majority of loyal, home-grown supporters – remains a very special occasion.

Which is all very lovely, but quite why it was decided that the final of the League Two play-offs between Northampton Town and Exeter City should be played on a Monday teatime behind closed doors and at goodness knows what cost to all involved takes some fathoming out. Inevitably, in the tradition of Dave Burnley, lifelong Cobblers' fan Don (no surname supplied) travelled from Ealing to stand outside during the game (you could have watched it on the telly, Don). BBC's James Law's report, trying desperately to squeeze some positivity out of the whole thing, concluded that without supporters, 'the overriding feeling was one of nothingness'. None of which would have deflated the joy in the households of Northampton as their team handed out a 4-0 spanking to their opponents. Let's just hope the M5 was clear for the Exeter contingent.

No doubt the journey back to Northampton was much jollier. The social distancing, which seemed a mixed bag at best while games were taking place, completely went out of the window at the end of the game as players embraced each other and their manager Keith Curle – one of the six BAME managers in the top four divisions. By the time he was nursing a restorative cup of coffee next morning, he was one of five.

Sulzeer Jeremiah, Sol, Campbell left his job as manager of Southend United by mutual consent. Throughout his career as a footballer and, by default, someone in public life, Sol Campbell has found himself at the centre of controversy. As a player he committed the cardinal offence of moving from one club to its major rival – Tottenham to Arsenal – and, what's more, refused to be apologetic or conciliatory about it in any way. 'My decision was totally based on football,' he explained. Arsenal were a 'great team, a great manager, great players. The set-up is geared to win.' And win trophies and titles he did, while his former colleagues strove unsuccessfully to do so. All of this played into a frenzied and truth-free impression of what Campbell was like.

His quiet and sometimes reserved nature, along with an unwillingness to share information about his private life, played into an infantile fiction that he must be gay. It was an idea that persisted with the puerile. In January 2019, while managing Macclesfield Town, he was subject to persistent abuse from that inferno of football madness that is Cheltenham Town. While praising the official reactions from both clubs, Campbell was unequivocal in his condemnation of the perpetrators: 'I think it's a sad affair to have this vile noise chanted at me with no remorse to how my wife, children and I must feel.'

Although such commentary about Campbell's sexuality did not surface in the coverage of his departure in the local press and in comments by Southend fans, there was a pretty unsubtle message about this supposed aloofness running through their discourse. 'Speak to those inside the club,' explained the *Basildon, Canvey and Southend Echo*, 'and a lack of communication would also often be the biggest criticism of Campbell's regime.' On Twitter, supporters maintained a level of courtesy but the strain of criticism was ubiquitous: 'aloof, cryptic and not a good communicator', according to wessexblue1; 'a strange character – arrogant and not what the club needed', suggested djm_eightyone;

'did himself no favours with his apparent distancing from the club's players and supporters', shrimpersaway informed us.

It is, of course, the inalienable right of every football supporter to express forthright views about how his or her club is run – and nothing that is said need have any relation to what actually happens behind the closed doors of that club and its affairs. Such criticism is even more justified if that well-informed critic is either a season-ticket holder or a regular attender at games. False impressions, dramatised narratives, the elevation of tittle-tattle to iron truths, are all part of the brilliant landscape of how football operates and, of course, sells itself back to the people who really should own it. One imagines that most of those who hold prominent positions in the game have developed mechanisms for blanking out all but the most egregious of insults and vilification that comes their way. But I think if I were Sol Campbell, my patience would be wearing pretty thin by now.

For someone with a reputation for aloofness, Campbell could hardly be deemed a shrinking violet. With over 500 league appearances and 73 England caps on his CV, he felt himself properly entitled to speak out on a range of views. In 2015 he expressed an interest, which turned out to be short-lived, in standing as a Conservative candidate for the London mayoral elections. He saw his political inexperience as no obstacle. In a foretaste of almost universal comment about politicians during the pandemic, he observed that he looked 'at people who have been in politics for five, ten, 15 years, and muck up, you see them muck up and think, "You guys are supposed to be pro!"'

In terms of identifying the issue of racism in football, he showed an equal lack of reserve, say openly that he believed he would have captained England on a regular basis had he been white. In October 2013 he raised the hackles of many observers by immediately criticising the FA's newly appointed commission into improving the national team. The eight-person (well, let's not beat about the bush, eight-man) commission was all white. 'You can't have similar people, similar mindsets, in one committee if you want to expand and find different solutions,' he argued. In more recent interviews, he has dared to bring the notion of unconscious bias into a footballing world previously resistant to such fancy notions. Although the EFL's adaption of a version of the Rooney Rule, whereby a BAME candidate must be interviewed for a managerial vacancy, represents some progress, the stubbornness of the cossetted and entitled Premier League in failing to do so – particularly at a time when their teams sported the Black Lives Matter slogan on their shirts – would have been particularly irksome.

In discussion about race and, to a lesser extent, class, football held up a mirror to much of what was happening in people's lives. Throughout the pandemic, the spectre of job loss and uncertain futures haunted millions of people. What also became clear was that all victims of Covid were not equal and that lockdown was experienced in a range of ways. And what was startlingly apparent was that issues of class, poverty and race ran through the entire experience. Work at home if you can, we were told, begging the question as to how a shelf stacker, delivery driver or refuse collector was going to achieve this. Isolate yourself if you have symptoms was the instruction. In a small flat with no garden and a family to support? Take regular exercise but maintain social distance – which is fine if you've got open parkland near your house, not so good if you're in the middle of a city housing estate. Want a test for Covid? Good luck with that.

By 20 May, the Premier League had invested over £4 million on testing. A few days earlier, the Prime Minister told the country and the House of Commons that a 'world class' test-and-trace system would be in place by 1 June. While we all waited to see evidence of this, football tested 748 employees at its top level with six positive cases across three clubs. For the rest of the nation, locating information about testing stations, eligibility and reliability still dogged the whole issue. As for apps, lost tests results, unmonitored self-isolation, U-turns on quarantine and mask wearing, these became the focus for derision in a thousand WhatsApp memes. For the 500 or so people needed to stage a televised football match, the ready availability of such testing on a very regular basis brought the shortcomings of government action into sharp relief.

On testing, as with so much, football held up a mirror to wider society at the start of July. As it happens, the new blue wall of Conservative seats in the north skirted round Wigan, where local MP Lisa Nandy realised what most followers of the game had known for a very long time when she said that 'there are serious questions to be asked about the EFL's processes'. Wigan itself, with an unemployment rate prior to Covid just below the national average – 3.5 per cent compared to 3.8 per cent – enjoys a degree of insulation from the worst effects of austerity and economic deprivation. Quite how the potential demise of the club would have an effect in the future was unclear. Meanwhile, down in the relatively affluent south, workers at the FA looked down the barrel at the unthinkable prospect of being transformed from valued employee to claimant. And while BLM logos proliferated and a welcome new public consciousness was cultivated, one of the six black managers in top-level football decided it wasn't for him.

Things might not have been falling apart. In some ways they may even have been getting slightly better – but sometimes it all felt, at best, like a work in progress. Once our gaze settled on clubs below the top two levels, those where the telly had at least provided some temporary financial relief, everything looked a touch more precarious.

Chapter 6

League One. Tranmere. Done by a decimal point

On the Saturday before Christmas 2019, Tranmere Rovers of League One, the third tier of English football, won 1-0 at home against Wimbledon. The victory took them just out of the relegation zone, now limited to three clubs with the demise of Bury; effectively this was really two, because of the 12-point penalty imposed on hapless Bolton. In the following 11 games they acquired just three points before achieving three wins on the trot, starting with victory at Shrewsbury on 25 February. Although still in the relegation places, this sudden spurt of form took them within three points of Wimbledon who were just above the safety line, although Rovers had a game in hand. Of their ten games scheduled once Covid halted matters, at least three could have been deemed to be against relegation rivals. There may have been just a glimmer of optimism, but everyone connected with the club was now aware that if the season finished there and then, with a system of points per game used to settle things, they would be relegated by 0.04 of a point.

To be entirely honest, I haven't double-checked the arithmetic of that calculation. I have always taken it on trust from the statements of Tranmere chairman, Mark Palios. There aren't many chairmen/women of football clubs to whom I would defer so easily – but this guy is a touch different.

For a start – and I concede that this isn't high science – he is referred to on Tranmere fans' forums as Mark. I wouldn't wish to calculate the number of hours I have lost trawling through such sites – and that includes my own club's – but I'd like to bet that a familiar and easy use of the chairman's forename, as opposed to some vitriolic, sneering slur, is far from the norm. Unlike many of the game's senior public figures, Mark Palios is absolutely steeped in football. In two spells with Tranmere spanning a dozen years, he played over 250 games for the club, as well as fitting in over 100 for nearby Crewe. He then turned out for Southport and Bangor, for whom he played in the European Cup Winners' Cup.

In an irritating display of all-round talent, he combined his playing achievements with success in accountancy, acquiring a partnership at Pricewaterhouse

Coopers. In 2003 he became chief executive of the Football Association and from there assumed a number of leadership roles for a range of sporting bodies. He has been voted Turnaround Financier of the Year – which I'll concede does sound a touch vainglorious – and in 2014 he and his wife assumed a controlling interest in Tranmere Rovers. The club had just been relegated to the fourth division and Palios's intervention could not prevent a further drop to the National League a year later. Three years at this fifth level ended with two consecutive promotions to League One where they found themselves struggling to keep up by March 2020. So, Palios's credentials are significantly more impressive than many of the 'blazers' – shorthand for the conservative plodders at the EFL – and those of some of his counterparts in the league. In short, if he says it's 0.04 of a point, I'm inclined to believe him.

For most football people, particularly those of a certain generation, Tranmere Rovers means two things: Friday night football and Johnny King and his 'trip to the moon'. For the best part of three decades starting in the 70s, Rovers, aware of the competing attraction of nearby Everton and Liverpool, chose to play on Friday nights. Their current fans observe that it's the question most frequently asked of them: 'Do your lot still play on Friday?' The vagaries of modern life, the immovable fatball of traffic that is the Friday night motorway experience and the prospect of (slightly) more glamorous football on TV saw the end of the tradition, although Palios was instrumental in bringing it back for a handful of local games from 2018. Its quirky place in the picture of England's football may yet return if, as seems possible, one of the outcomes of potential restructuring is a more localised league set-up.

As for Johnny King, one can only imagine that if he had plied his trade higher up the football ladder, he would have enjoyed the same sort of celebrity status as Clough or Shankly – he was, in fact, dubbed Tranmere's Bill Shankly by the *Liverpool Echo* – such was the outlandishness of his comments and actions. Former Tranmere captain Eric Nixon once told a journalist that during King's spell as manager, he had called him in and told him that the troops needed rallying. 'What I want you to do now,' King instructed, 'is go back to that squad and tell each and every player to grab an oar and row as hard as they can for the shore. I want them all to be like Kirk Douglas in that movie, *The Vikings*.' It was, apparently, just another day at the office and nothing to be alarmed about.

Like Palios, King was steeped in the club. He played for them 250 times, mostly as captain in the 1960s, and had two spells as manager between 1975 and 1980 and 1987 and 1996. It was in this latter period that he almost took a club that had played exclusively in the lower two divisions of the professional game to within touching distance of the moon – the Premier League. Having gained promotion to the second tier, Tranmere reached the play-offs on three occasions between 1993 and 1995, beaten in the semi-finals on each occasion. They did reach Wembley twice, once successfully, in the final of the variously sponsored cup for lower division clubs. In 1994, only a penalty shoot-out prevented them from reaching the League Cup Final. They built a reputation as a fearless, attacking side and when King moved upstairs from the dugout in 1996, he was replaced by Liverpool legend John Aldridge as manager. In 2002 he was afforded one of football's most prized accolades when the Borough Road Stand was named after him. The anniversary of his death in 2016 is still marked by Rovers supporters.

But the Friday night tradition, the hero that was Johnny King and the considerable expertise and acumen of Mark Palios counted for nothing when, on 9 June, the EFL issued an 86-word statement on its website informing readers that 'an overwhelming majority' of clubs had agreed to end the season and that accordingly 'Tranmere Rovers ... will start the 2020/21 season in League Two'. Search around their website for as long as you like, the 86 words are all you're going to find. Some days prior to this curt communication, Palios had submitted a closely argued six-page document arguing for a nuanced approach that involved some football for those clubs still in with a chance of deciding their fate on the field of play. It cut no ice.

The tone of the online reaction to the EFL's decision was one of resigned sorrow rather than anger. In an almost statesmanlike response given the circumstances, Palios posted a statement on the club's website in which he conceded that the pandemic had foisted a particularly difficult task on the game's ruling body. There was, however, no disguising the bitterness of some of his remarks. 'It cannot be right,' he observed, 'that clubs are pitted against clubs, when nobody voting (including Tranmere) is able to take a purely dispassionate view. Perhaps it exposes the fable of the "football family" and the complete collapse of the collective when faced with an external challenge.' In an unsurprising sideswipe at some of his fellow chairmen, he was dismissive of those 'who have sympathised at the unfairness of our plight, whilst still voting for it … sympathy doesn't pay wages or assuage a deep sense of unfairness'. In a separate, shorter statement on the site a day later, the club expressed its regret for the 20 redundancies it would be forced to make at the end of July.

Those 20 redundancies featured frequently in comments on Tranmere fans' forums as debate about the EFL's decision developed. A legal challenge, even if successful, would be a drain on the club's finances and resources. If it failed – and it would have been difficult to envisage any other outcome – the ramifications would have been practically unthinkable, especially for those whose livings remained on the line. Discussion threads gradually seemed to morph into an interestingly repetitive format: this is an unfair decision and I am furious; it's probably not worth appealing against so we have to suck it up; football is run by a bunch of self-seeking morons; what changes do you reckon we'll need to the squad once we do eventually get playing again?

At the start of June 2020, Tranmere Rovers Football Club, soon to find itself back in League Two, looked into the middle distance and tried, in vain, to see the shape of the future. That future didn't look any brighter when, on 7 July, manager Micky Mellon accepted a new job at Dundee United. I have no wish to alienate a significant proportion of my readership by asking a mischievous question as to whether Mellon had advanced his career by moving from the fourth tier of the English game to a newly promoted team from the second in Scotland; I'll leave that there for the pointless sort of debate that diverts us all. Dundee United had established a clear lead in the Scottish Championship when a halt was called to proceedings and, what's more, were a whopping 18 points clear of their neighbours a few yards further down Tannadice Street. *The Courier* – trusted news, photos and videos from Dundee, Fife, Perth and Angus

– made its position clear when it predicted 'grim times for Dundee fans'.

To say that Tranmere and its supporters acted with grace and dignity when faced with the departure of a much-loved part of their set-up, especially in an age of unregulated keyboard fury, is an understatement. Dundee United's sporting director, Tony Asghar, paid tribute to the 'professional and respectful manner during negotiations' exhibited by Mark Palios, who, in his turn, seemed to comment without rancour on Mellon's departure. Acknowledging that it was 'a sad note on which to leave', Palios expressed total confidence that Mellon would have kept the club up had the season not been truncated. 'I am disappointed that Micky wished to move on,' he explained, 'but, as a Scot, the opportunity to manage in the Scottish Premier League was one which was too good for him to miss and I did not feel it was right to stand in his way.'

Similar courtesy was evident on forums. Pete SF captured it succinctly: 'A great job, three Wembley appearances, two promotions. You done Tranmere proud. Good luck in your new post.' And then, with the absolute inevitability of football fans and their outlook, the speculation started about Mellon's replacement.

The comprehensive study has yet to be done about how football supporters in the 21st century conduct their discussions about future managers. I should be able to remember what happened in pre-social media days, but I can't. I suspect that the reason for this is that it may have been discussed at workplaces and in clubs and pubs, but the jangle of modern speculation – most of it idle but harmless – was entirely absent. And, of course, it just didn't happen that often. In contrast, a skim through the last complete survey and report by the League Managers Association (LMA) shows that in the season ending in 2018, there were 54 dismissals of managers across the 92 clubs with a further 11 resignations. The average tenure at any one club was 1.18 years. The LMA's records only go back to 2005 – when there were 40 sackings – and although there is no discernible pattern, numbers have hovered between 31 and 58 ever since. So, whichever lens you look through, most managers might want to think twice about elaborate office decorations in an industry where they have something like a 60 per cent chance of being out on their ear within a matter of months.

On top of that, the betting industry, which has attached itself like a stubborn burr to football, enthusiastically feeds the speculation and chatter. Worth £349 million in shirt sponsorship in the Premier League alone, and with 17 Championship teams bearing gambling logos, 27 of the top 44 teams have their fortunes mixed up with the industry. In the first month of the pandemic, according to the Gambling

Commission, the betting firms took a bit of a hit – but it was just a bit. Punters had fewer live events to entice them and income from that sector dropped by 55 per cent – or £100 million – between March and April. But stem your tears. Online slots, poker and betting on virtual events made up some £15 million of that shortfall and by the end of May, way before Ray Winstone could pop up on our screens with his faux gangster act and growl at us to gamble responsibly, expenditure on harmless – and not so harmless – fluttering was nearly back to pre-lockdown levels. Only in such a climate could the Sack Race betting site prosper, offering odds on all the usual suspects for every vacancy, real and imagined. Micky Mellon's departure installed John McGreal from Colchester United as their immediate odds-on favourite. They turned out to be wrong. Ten days after Mellon set off for Scotland, Tranmere appointed former assistant Mike Jackson. McGreal parted company with Colchester a few weeks later with the principal rumour being that he was about to take Sol Campbell's place at Southend. The Sack Race reported him as a plump 14/1 for the job.

In the middle of all of this, I manage to speak to someone who works for the club's community department. As with all clubs during this post-lockdown period, it's hard to get hold of people. In a reflection of the times, many of those who answer phones, doing nuts-

and-bolts jobs involved in day-to-day administration, are either furloughed or working on a very part-time basis. This is, of course, a situation that is even more pronounced in the lower reaches of the league pyramid. Given that by mid-July we are in a prolonged close season for clubs like Tranmere, there is a strong sense of things being necessarily, if temporarily, mothballed. With the lack of certainty about the 2020/21 season, this is completely unsurprising.

Nevertheless, a representative of the club's community department and I have a lively and amicable chat. She tells me of how, during lockdown, the club's activities had been energetically devoted to working with the local community. Acting as a sort of triage department, sorting out calls and requests for help, Rovers worked closely with charitable organisations to deliver shopping and prescriptions as well as organising a befriending scheme. She talks with pride of being a genuine community club, noting that 'to be fair, most clubs that I know about will have been doing their bit'. Workers furloughed from the club and the wider community have been pleased to volunteer their services. It's a reflection of the surge of volunteering in the country which saw three-quarters of a million people sign up for the NHS Volunteer Scheme as well as a whole range of other ways of working with those in need in their localities.

When it comes to talking about next season, she sighs deeply. Like me, she can't see any possibility of crowds being in grounds until October at the earliest. Even then, it is difficult to envisage what that would look like. 'We really need fans coming back,' she tells me. 'We're not like any of those clubs who can survive without that income.' Despite the fact that socially distanced spectators might just be an outside possibility at grounds like Prenton Park, emerging concerns about supplying a range of other facilities, of which toilet use is just about the most down to earth and persistent, remains a problem. As for hospitality and catering, both significant contributors to revenue, both look likely to be on hold for a while.

I was pleased that I managed to speak to someone at the club. Significantly, this person wanted to remain anonymous because of uncertainty about 'whether the chairman would approve'. This appeared to be part of a pattern. Approaches to the club's media department were met with polite, but insistent, rebuffs. Attempts to communicate with Mark Palios himself were greeted with complete radio silence until he sent me an extremely courteous text in the middle of August, the contents of which confirmed that this reticence on the part of the club was part of a clear strategy.

On 4 August, a comprehensive 17-minute interview with Palios had been posted on the club's website.

'Football people' are often overly coy in their public statements, particularly when it comes to their own clubs, careful not to stray from the corporate line. This was definitely not the approach of the chairman of Tranmere Rovers as he addressed online all the things I would have asked him had I spoken to him in person. Informing everything, he said, was one solid, old-fashioned maxim: if you've got nothing to say, keep your mouth shut. The balance between 'communicating or not' had to fall on the side of only giving information that is useful or accurate. At a time when planning was 'impossible', Palios had made the sensible decision not to hold out false promise.

'We rely on playing gates,' he explained. Everyone is talking about a return on 12 September, but with the emergence of local lockdowns 'who knows if this is feasible?' As to the likelihood of crowds in grounds, only 'the health of people can decide' if such a thing would be possible. When it comes to the buying and selling of players, the club needs to be cautious. A potential salary cap – and it's instructive that an insider like Palios should even mention this – could potentially see clubs falling foul of the rules and being deducted points. He is cautious about 'rescue packages' from the game's authorities, which could turn out to be burdensome loans. He uses the colourful expression of being in a 'free universe' to capture the prevailing uncertainty. Against such a background, he is not prepared to gamble on the stability that has been brought to the club in the last six years: 'Whatever we do, we'll do properly. We need to balance the need to take chances in an uncertain marketplace and remain agile at the same time.'

He is intensely proud of the work done in the community and of fundraising that has approached £50,000. He cites the example of players who have left the club who often mention its links with the local community as one of the things they associate with Tranmere. Palios talks with genuine and obvious warmth about engaging with the people who are at the centre of the club and who have expressed the strength of this connection by their involvement in a range of activities from the shirt-design competition to their voluntary work in the upkeep of Prenton Park. He wants to repay that loyalty by scrapping all deadlines when it comes to deals over the purchase of season tickets. After all, he explains, 'the reality is that nobody can tell me when we will allow those people to come into the ground to watch a game of football'.

He expresses the hope that his actions, even his unwillingness to speak if there is nothing to say, will have the effect of building further trust with supporters. 'I don't like to ask people to trust me because I'd rather they see what we do,' he suggests, before going on to say that if there had been 'one good thing about Covid', it was that everybody had been able to 'see the strength of the club once again'. In the meantime, the focus is on the return to playing football. Training, with all its associated costs, has just started and manager 'Jacko' is fully installed. Safety protocols are dictating everything that happens and the club's employees, like the rest of society, are looking carefully and sensibly at returning to something approaching normal. Everything is in place … and here he uses an interesting expression … 'in case we return on 12 September'.

In case. That just about captured where we were at the start of August 2020.

League One. Points per game as one bead on the abacus does for Tranmere.

		Games played	Points	Goal difference
1.	Coventry	34	67	18
2.	Rotherham	35	62	23
3.	Wycombe	34	59	5
4.	Oxford	35	60	24
5.	Portsmouth	35	60	17
6.	Fleetwood	35	60	13
7.	Peterborough	35	59	28
8.	Sunderland	36	59	16
9.	Doncaster	34	54	18
10.	Gillingham	35	51	8
11.	Ipswich	36	52	10
12.	Burton	35	48	0
13.	Blackpool	35	45	1
14.	Bristol Rovers	35	45	-11
15.	Shrewsbury	34	41	-11
16.	Lincoln	35	42	-2
17.	Accrington St.	35	40	-6
18.	Rochdale	34	36	-18
19.	MK Dons	35	37	-11
20.	Wimbledon	35	35	-13
21.	Tranmere	34	32	-24
22.	Southend	35	19	-46
23.	Bolton	35	14	-39
24.	Bury	0	0	0

Bolton deducted 12 points prior to the season. Bury ceased to operate before the season started.

Chapter 7

League Two. The clue's in the name. Forest Green – the sustainable club that aims to be made of wood

On 12 January 2020, Forest Green Rovers were in seventh place in League Two, the fourth tier of English football. They had acquired 44 points from 27 games, the same number as four other clubs, although they had played a game or two more than some around them. Swindon – almost neighbours at 30 miles from FGR's home at Nailsworth – looked uncatchable and turned out to be league winners when the season finished in June, decided on a points-per-game basis. But in January, a place in the play-offs was a possibility and the chairman, Dale Vince, was able to talk optimistically about the ambition of being in League One, housed in their new, wooden Eco Park.

But when football ground to a halt in March, FGR had scraped a mere five points from the ensuing ten games and any remote possibility of a charge at the play-offs had all but vanished.

The club's official website provided a window into the effects of the virus at this level of the game. An official statement posted on 24 March informed supporters that the government's furlough scheme would be used for all FGR staff and that the club was investigating how best to support its casual employees. It went on to warn that there would 'be minimal social updates on all of our channels' before wishing supporters well and urging them to keep safe. This headline story stayed in place until 12 June when it was replaced by information about arrangements for season-ticket refunds. It was followed on 15 June by news about which players would be released by the club. The other main story, rather than alleviating the gloom, seemed to reinforce the notion of an establishment frantically chasing reasons to be cheerful: the cook-off that was the Great Quorn Tikka Masala Challenge.

Because that, of course, is what most fans who know anything at all about Forest Green Rovers can tell you: you can't get a pie there. Or if you can, it's some veggie aberration made from beans and seeds. In that, as in almost everything about it, the club is a reflection of the life and character of Dale Vince.

Vince, like Mark Palios at Tranmere, is an extraordinary man. Whether the clash of two such energetic forces contributes to the rivalry discussed shortly can only be guesswork. Having left school at 15 and after working as a mechanic, he took to the road in his 20s and his various wanderings led him into homespun experimentations with wind power. To be exact, he put a turbine of sorts on top of his ex-army lorry. Driven as he was by a commitment to his new-age, eco-friendly projects, and despite his assertion that he is still 'this slightly crazy hippy bloke' that he was in the early 90s, when it comes to financial acumen, Vince is a shark, not a minnow. In 1996, he founded the green energy firm, Ecotricity, and was unfazed by an attempt at commercial piracy by the giant entity, Tesla, who he accused of attempting to filch his company's intellectual property.

He may have been prepared to put his body on the line at environmental protests but when it comes to hard-headed business, Vince knows the rules. Interviewed in *The Independent* in 2014, he scotched the idea that there was any conflict of values between his green activist credentials and making money. Don't be fooled, he told the paper, 'we're not a not-for-profit organisation'. If the point needed further proving, Vince found himself on *The Sunday Times* Rich List but in doing so, was insistent that he remained driven by values as well as revenue: 'Most people in the country judge success by how much money you've made, so if my success gives renewable energy credibility, then that's great.'

Chapter 2 of this book reminded us of the days when a businessman with an eye on installing himself in his local club as chairman (and make no mistake, there would have been none of the gender neutrality of chairperson) would have been a version, admittedly not always as colourful, of Bob Lord – who was, just to remind ourselves, a butcher by trade. One can only relish the wonderful fantasy of what Bob the Butcher's generation would have made of Vince the Vegan. Having become a major shareholder of FGR in 2010 he went on to become chairman and within a year, the sale of all red meat was banned at the ground and, what's more, from the players' diets. Various innovations followed: solar panels for all energy; an organic pitch; solar-powered, robotic grass cutting and, eventually – and with a certain inevitability – the declaration in 2015 that FGR was an all-vegan football club.

This acquisition of this genuinely unique status took place in the same year that the club achieved a position from which it might just have found itself in the Football League for the first time in its history. In the first of three consecutive seasons in which the club appeared in the National League play-offs, they fell at the semi-final stage to Bristol Rovers, before getting beaten in the final at Wembley by Grimsby the following season and then, eventually, getting it right by beating Tranmere in the final in 2017. Yes, that's right: they beat their great rivals in the final.

Football throws up some unlikely rivalries and historic animosities. On my first visit to Wycombe's Adams Park out of nerdy curiosity some years ago, I was taken aback to hear the usual banal bile being directed to their great rivals … Colchester United. Just google it: it makes no sense at all. Stevenage supporters reserve their greatest indignation for Woking and Boston harbour a deep grudge against Dagenham and Redbridge. I'm not making the case that the Rovers of Tranmere and Forest Green are holding on to anything quite as peculiar, but the evil that is Twitter certainly stirred up a spat that bought out the infantile worst in elements from both clubs as lockdown ended.

Dale Vince was unimpressed with the plan hatched by his fellow chairman, Mark Palios, for ending the season and was unequivocal, but not particularly discourteous, in how he expressed this view. 'Surprised to read this,' he tweeted on 2 June. 'Tranmere's proposal is complex and looks designed specifically for their circumstances – to avoid relegation. I see no equity or logic in it.' When the decision of the 0.04 was eventually reached, he proclaimed it a victory for common sense. It did not endear him to the citizenry of Birkenhead. It may just have been that a tweet earlier in May in which Vince expressed the view that they'd be meeting next season had spiced matters up a little, and so there followed the usual bilge and bovine exchanges through which Twitter has so improved the world. From a neutral perspective, it was a touch unsettling to witness a club chairman engaging in such yah-boo sucks stuff in the middle of a global pandemic – a point that many Tranmere fans were happy to point out – but teacups and storms just about covers it.

With the dust from this skirmish settled, Forest Green Rovers, a football club enjoying a past characterised by success in the lower reaches of English football, who had enjoyed appearances and victories in the FA Vase and Trophy, who had been to Wembley (and Villa Park) in those finals and whose mark on the game was being made in ways that would have had Bob Lord hacking at the brisket in confused fury, finished the season in good old mid-table anonymity. What was going to come next was anyone's guess, but in the meantime, FGR decided to sleep it out.

Whether it was the club's closeness to nature or just a random linguistic choice, it decided to characterise itself as 'going into hibernation'. In a statement in May it informed supporters that it would be using the government's furlough scheme to ensure that employees would be kept on and their salaries protected up to

£2,500 per month. A media release explained that 'our staff have been unable to work since the shutdown. This decision recognises that and puts the club into hibernation.' It went on to make clear that there would be 'minimal social updates on all of our channels until we're open and football is back'. It is intended as no criticism whatsoever to observe that the club was true to its word. Phone lines were dead and attempts to use any social media to speak to anyone connected to the club were met with silence. This wasn't discourtesy; it was plain business sense. What's more, as lockdown began to ease in July, Forest Green Rovers showed itself to be a club that really did know how to communicate with its public.

On 24 July, CEO Henry Staelens, to whom I had spoken briefly a few days previously, issued a comprehensive and informative statement on the club's website. Staff, including casual and matchday staff, had all been paid 100 per cent of their salaries. Season tickets would not be on sale until the club knew what was happening in terms of admitting spectators but some promising players had been signed. The club was going cashless and the new away strip was on sale. There would be pre-season friendlies but it was highly unlikely that fans would be able to attend. Clear, honest and useful information and in the middle of it, an obvious indication of the direction of travel of a club informed by a hard-headed business outlook. Forest Green Rovers was going to go as digital as it could.

Henry Staelens's comments talked of a structural reorganisation at the club and even of taking on 'new starters'. The majority of these, he informed us, 'will join our revamped media setup, becoming the Content Team, allowing us to produce and deliver more digital stories for you throughout each season'. The quality of such work was about to go 'up a few notches' alongside a rebuilt website, fans' forum and 'perhaps most excitingly, an FGR app which will be a real game changer for supporters'. Forest Green may have been hibernating, but they'd been dreaming big about what post-Covid digitised football might be looking like for its followers.

In the same spirit of clarity and openness, the club issued a comprehensive statement from its Head of Medical, Ian Weston, on 29 July. Expressing the view that the 'players have returned in good shape' but with safety as the priority, we were informed that they would need to fill in a daily questionnaire, have their temperature checked and to turn up to training in their own kit, bringing their own food. And, of course, they would be tested regularly. When it came to this element, Ian Weston did not hold back; it's an uncomfortable business. They'll have swabs 'stuck down the back of their throats and up their nose to determine whether or not' they are infected. Such tests will be carried out on a regular basis at 'no cost to the UK taxpayer' with the club paying the bill. The statement continues with a clear and precise outline of steps to be taken should infection be detected and steps for readmittance. It concludes with the bold assertion that 'currently there is no scientific evidence for reinfection'.

Maybe not such a bold comment. Three weeks earlier, the journal *Science* reported on research with macaques, the mammal most closely mimicking humans, which furnished observers' cause for limited optimism when it came to reinfection and immunity. It reached conclusions that, according to the USA's National Institute for Health:

> ... *lend hope that COVID-19 patients who develop acquired immunity may be at low risk for reinfection, at least in the short term. Additional studies are underway to track people who came down with COVID-19 in New York during March and April to see if any experience reinfection. By the end of this year, we should have better answers.*

In this, the research mirrored the hopes of everyone that some sort of herd immunity, a concept discredited through its clumsy use by the government early in the piece, may yet develop and so let us back into football grounds. Oh yes, and go to school, work and generally get us out and about to revive a ruined economy.

Over on the fans' forum, this emergence from hibernation was met with appreciative enthusiasm. Old Tom Cat purred that the club had 'been working hard behind the scenes – all good stuff' and this was echoed in other comments. Bill Shankly – no clue as to the relevance of the moniker – saw a wider issue, reflected in conversations taking place everywhere: it's great that players and staff are safe, but when are we all going to get reliable testing and some sort of track-and-trace system that even vaguely works? 'It's the only way to eradicate it,' argues Bill. For all of that, it is the impending departure of captain and star player Joseph Mills, probably to one of the promoted clubs and, most irksomely, possibly to Swindon Town, that generates the most traffic. Eight players have been signed, but Mills's departure seems to be taken as something of a sign of the times. Manager Mark Cooper talks about how 'in the current climate everyone is cutting their cloth a bit', going on to observe that with the player out of contract 'and someone offering another £500 a week and he wants to move his family, there's nothing we can do about that'.

In the week prior to the start of the 2020/21 season, Dale Vince's management team endeavoured to set me up with an interview with him, but his wide range of commitments prevented this from happening. CEO Henry Staelens stepped in once again at the start of September and, in a feat of admirable professionalism and diplomacy, managed to keep quiet about a major piece of news that was to break within hours. Arsenal's Spanish defender, Héctor Bellerín, announced that he was to become the club's second largest shareholder. 'So many people feel there are no solutions to the world's problems,' he told the BBC, 'but Forest Green are already doing plenty.' Having already raised funds for the planting of 60,000 trees in the Amazon rainforest, Bellerín's green credentials had been well established. 'I like Héctor's approach,' Dale Vince explained approvingly. 'I'm looking forward to working with him on FGR and this wider agenda we have a shared interest in.'

This acknowledgement of a wider agenda is apparent in everything Henry Staelens talks about. In a world in which 'many club owners are a danger to themselves', he is proud that FGR has brought 'a different conversation to football' in a way that is prepared to challenge a stale image of 'meat pies and pints'. If some good is to come out of the pandemic, it must reside in a willingness to think about sustainability on all levels, from the economic to the environmental. There needs to be a sense of collective responsibility in everything from the acceptance of salary caps to financial planning that can sustain beyond the next 13 weeks.

As far as the immediate future is concerned, the club is planning for the possibility of limited entrance of season-ticket holders, although he acknowledges that with a fan base that tends towards the older – and hence more cautious – end of the age spectrum, and with three sides of the ground being standing only, it will be a challenge to both entice people back to football and to keep them socially distanced. When I put it to him that there is growing evidence that people are itching to get back to watching football and that the club may even be the beneficiary of exiles from bigger clubs, he's a touch unconvinced, but happy to be proved wrong. 'We're not in a big football area. We're working hard to get as many as we can from anywhere!'

Who knows? Maybe the stardust sprinkled from Héctor Bellerín may make the club's light shine brighter still in the game's firmament. Perhaps a vision of sustainability, rooted in a local community and driven by the notion of working towards a collective good, might prove just the antidote to the bloated selfishness of the game at elite level. If the game as we know it has its roots in the powerful industries located in large towns and cities, maybe it will learn to coexist with different models, in different places and with different values. As we learnt from Covid, the unthinkable and the unimaginable does happen. The football world might just be a brighter and more diverse place with a club like open-minded Forest Green Rovers in the vanguard.

League Two. Forest Green nestle anonymously but a sweat for Stevenage, who survive after winning just three times thanks to the EFL's bizarre procedures. An agonising drop for Macclesfield. Seventh place good enough for Northampton Town.

Final position		Games played	Points	Goal difference
1.	Swindon	36	69	23
2.	Crewe	37	69	24
3.	Plymouth	37	68	22
4.	Cheltenham	36	64	25
5.	Exeter	37	65	10
6.	Colchester	37	58	15
7.	Northampton	37	58	14
8.	Port Vale	37	57	6
9.	Bradford City	37	54	4
10.	Forest Green	36	49	3
11.	Salford	37	50	3
12.	Walsall	36	47	-9
13.	Crawley	37	48	4
14.	Newport	36	46	-7
15.	Grimsby	37	47	-6
16.	Cambridge Utd	37	45	-8
17.	Leyton Orient	36	42	-8
18.	Carlisle	37	42	-17
19.	Oldham	37	41	-13
20.	Scunthorpe	37	40	-12
21.	Mansfield	36	38	-7
22.	Morecambe	37	32	-25
23.	Stevenage	36	22	-26
24.	Macclesfield*	37	19	-15

* Macclesfield deducted a total of 17 points over the season relating to three different disciplinary cases.

Chapter 8

National League.
Solihull Moors wait it out
with sanitiser and season-
ticket deals

A few days after the announcement that the fifth division of English football was calling it a day, the season well and truly ended for Solihull Moors. Barrow had been promoted to the Football League as champions with the six clubs below them entering a convoluted play-off system. Two points adrift from entering the melee, Moors, like so many from the third tier downwards, had to think about planning for a future which was almost impossible to envisage.

In the second week of June, in a move obviously calculated to bring valuable revenue to the club, 500 season tickets were offered at genuine knock-down prices. £100 plus VAT got an adult into all 23 scheduled matches for the 2020/21 season; 16 to 18-year-olds could snap up the same bargain for £50 and under-16s would be admitted free if accompanying a full-paying adult or season-ticket holder. To put that into perspective, the walk-up price at Damson Park for an adult had been £18. Attendance prior to lockdown had fallen to the 700/800s. The offer of football at about a fiver a game – whatever and whenever that football might happen – looked an attractive proposition. In a bizarre twist, car-park season tickets were double the price at £200.

With no football stories with which to entertain their followers, the club energetically promoted a local enterprise, set up as not-for-profit, making hand sanitiser to support food banks and NHS workers. Beyond this, there was support for a breast cancer charity through the donation of face masks. The 'Moors 4 Challenge' – walking four miles every four hours for 24 hours – raised over £10,000 for the integration and education of excluded and vulnerable local people. Even allowing for a degree of company speak, a commitment to its community ran through everything that the club was trying to say about itself.

This laudable pledge to making a genuine contribution was made even more commendable when juxtaposed to the few, rather dispiriting references to the playing side of things. Sliding down the menu of the stories on the website were two that told of a club that, like so many enterprises and institutions in football and beyond, was looking to cut every penny of non-essential expenditure. The process had started in late April when all coaching and playing staff agreed to a 25 per cent wage cut. The directors and shareholders agreed a £20,000 donation to the Solihull Moors Foundation, dedicated to providing support for the local community.

Just over a week after this story was posted, the club issued a transparent picture of its playing resources. Of the 31 players at its disposal prior to the pandemic, nine remained under contract and four were in the process of renegotiating. Sixteen were out of contract or being released and two loanees were returning to parent clubs. Had the league's governing body decided to resume the season in full by mid-June – which, to be fair, was an unlikely prospect – Moors would have been doing so with a playing squad of 13 players. One of whom would not have been Darren Carter.

Readers will, I hope, excuse a touch of partisan localism here – especially as I have written about Darren in *Hugging Strangers*. Moors make a point of fostering relationships with neighbouring clubs in the Football League; season-ticket holders from Birmingham, Villa and West Brom are entitled to reduced admission at home games. So it will have been with genuine regret that Birmingham supporters in particular – he did endure a spell at West Brom as well – would have taken note of the playing demise of Darren Anthony Carter, Solihull born and bred, at the age of 36. He had clocked up over 300 appearances in the top divisions before moving on to play for Forest Green 62 times and then turning out for the Moors on over 100 occasions. He had represented England at junior levels a dozen times, a brush with minor glory which only received brief attention when he was dismissed for clattering Cristiano Ronaldo. No matter, for the blue side of Birmingham he was indelibly etched into history.

On the evening of Sunday, 12 May 2002, an 18-year-old Carter walked up to take the decisive penalty in the Championship play-off final in Cardiff – leaving many of his more senior contemporaries shrinking in the centre circle – and scored. It's fair to say that he never became the glowing superstar that his early form seemed to promise and even as a young man he looked as though he might benefit from some advice on calorie intake. By the time he was sedately controlling the midfield back in Solihull, convincingly enough to earn himself a place in the National League Team of the Season in 2019, he had taken to sporting guitar-hero flowing locks. Along with his increasing girth, he cut an unlikely, but effective, figure as a professional athlete. His unashamedly one-eyed performances as co-commentator on local radio served to enhance his status as an endearing nonconformist. (And to be fair, Darren,

I note from your post-lockdown appearances on Blues TV that quite a few pounds appear to have been shed.)

Solihull itself is something of a contested entity. Pointless but diverting arguments rumble on about whether it is a town in its own right, although given that it abuts major Birmingham suburbs, this seems faintly absurd. Those who cling to this idea of it being an exception probably base this assumption on the fact that Solihull has become synonymous with gentrified comfort in a well-to-do enclave beyond the rougher and readier parts of the city. There can be no disputing this when driving through the area's leafy boulevards, concealing spruce rows of gated mock Tudor dwellings. In contrast, the borough of Solihull encompasses the notorious township of Chelmsley Wood where the last official ward profile in 2016 identified the area as being one of the ten wards in the country suffering the most social and economic deprivation, according to the Index of Multiple Deprivation. The proximity of such want hasn't stopped successive generations of smug Brummies from disowning the city and insisting on telling you they're from So- lee- hull, if you don't mind.

It's also home to Solihull Jaguar Land Rover, the remaining outpost of the industry that was at the heart of the city for decades. On the edge of the factory sits Damson Park. With a capacity of just over 3,000, it lies five miles from St Andrew's and seven from Villa

Park. Its nearest neighbours in the National League are Notts County, some 43 miles away. Formed by an amalgamation between Solihull Borough and Moor Green FC in 2007, the club steadily established itself before achieving promotion to the National League in 2016. In keeping with the West Midlands tradition of dancing dangerously with relegation until the last minute, Moors pulled off a great escape of their own in 2018 under the managership of former England goalkeeper Tim Flowers, before enjoying their best season to date in 2018/19. With crowds then averaging over 1,300, they finished second in the league only to fall foul of the play-offs to AFC Fylde who, in their turn, were overturned by celebrity-endorsed Salford City in the final. With an FA Cup run that took them to the second round proper, Moors had established themselves as a viable and forward-looking part of the footballing landscape.

The chairman of the club is Darryl Eales, a man for whom the adjective 'irrepressible' might have been specifically coined. I speak to him the morning after Oxford United, where he had held a similar role until 2018, had been beaten by Wycombe in the League One play-off final at Wembley. Darryl had been present and with the eye of the board member as well as the fan, he admits that he felt 'gutted, but would have felt a lot worse if I'd owned the club'.

As it happens, he is a fan and, with me, shares the affliction that is Birmingham City. We enjoy the regulation grizzle that always occurs whenever two such victims meet, but Darryl is clear-headed about what he wants from Moors and his vision is unsurprising: 'I want to nick fans from Blues and Villa who have become disillusioned with football at that level and who want a bit of local involvement, a sense of perspective.' With a complete lack of rancour that is uncommon when Birmingham supporters comment on their rivals, he expresses his view that 'the only person hurting at Villa Park right now is Dean Smith – there's just not enough local people at the club'. It's a view that he reiterates when talking about Birmingham City who, he believes, have failed completely to engage with the local community – and it's an opinion that's hard to dispute when walking to games at St Andrew's and noting the utter indifference of the occasion to the local South Asian community. For Darryl, this is simply not an option when it comes to how Solihull Moors as a club conducts its affairs.

He expands on what I had already gleaned from the website about the club's commitment to its community during lockdown. Becci Fox, the club's Disability and Community Manager, had worked tirelessly with food banks in Chelmsley Wood; manager Jimmy Shan had used significant amounts of his time to talk to disadvantaged and isolated individuals; the club's project of producing face masks for free distribution had been a huge success. Darryl is particularly proud of how staff, even some of those who had become reliant on the Chancellor's rescue package, had dedicated time to the club: 'We were painting, moving, shifting rubbish – we were DIY furlough people.' Many of us learnt during the height of lockdown that, for the main part, it was bringing the best out of people. For unremittingly optimistic Darryl – 'this could be the land of opportunity for clubs with heart and ambition' – this was true in bucketloads.

If he had been animated when talking about how the club had coped during lockdown, he becomes positively evangelical when imagining the future – all of which is bound up with identifying Solihull Moors as more than the performance of the first team on Saturday and Tuesday. 'We see ourselves as a 24/7 community amenity enhanced by the 3G pitch, conference facilities and our involvement with the community.' While Darryl is clear that values are at the heart of how the club does its business, there is no disguising the hard edge of what he wants to achieve. Football is, after all, a competitive enterprise and far from shying away from this, it's at the heart of what he wants for Moors: 'How do we emerge as a club relatively stronger than any club in the division and, ultimately, how do we get to League One, which is where we want to be?'

He can't wait for the season to start and, as far as he can tell, he thinks this will be sometime in mid-September. As for all of us, peering into the misty future is a shaky business, but he sees it as a chance for football in general to 'reset the clock'. We talk of the demise and tribulations of those clubs who have fallen foul of feckless owners or dim-witted accountancy: he is damningly unsympathetic. He's been 'banging on about irresponsible ownership for years' and believes that penalties for going into administration – which he labels as 'gaming' for some clubs – or not paying wages, should be draconian, with relegation by three divisions the outcome. In terms of club ownership, he would prefer to see a more collective model involving a more diverse model of shareholders. Fans, too, he suggests, should learn to be more patient and tolerant.

I mention that my aim is to conclude each of my case studies of clubs coming out of lockdown by coming to see them as soon as any individuals external to clubs are allowed back as spectators. He immediately tells me to come along as his guest. As it happens, the wait to do so may turn out to be longer than anticipated. Shortly after the Premier League and the EFL announced that the new season was to kick off on 12 September, the National League informed their clubs that they would have to wait until 3 October – but with the tempting proposition of reduced crowds. When Darryl makes his offer, which he immediately reinforces by email, I tell him, probably infected by his powerful enthusiasm, that I can't wait – but I don't think I'm ready to be nicked from Blues after more than 60 years. I'm prepared to be wrong.

National League – settled by points per game.
Barrow back in the Football League after 48 years.
Convoluted play-offs reward second-place Harrogate. Moors sit on the rails and wait to stride on next season.

		Games played	*Points*	*Goal difference*
1.	Barrow	37	70	29
2.	Harrogate Town	37	66	17
3.	Notts County	38	63	23
4.	Yeovil Town	37	60	17
5.	Boreham Wood	37	60	15
6.	Halifax Town	37	58	1
7.	Barnet	35	54	-3
8.	Stockport County	39	58	6
9.	Solihull Moors	38	55	11
10.	Woking	38	55	-1
11.	Dover Athletic	38	54	0
12.	Hartlepool Utd	39	55	6
13.	Bromley	38	52	5
14.	Torquay Utd	36	48	-5
15.	Sutton Utd	38	50	5
16.	Eastleigh	37	46	-12
17.	Dagenham & R/brdge	37	44	-4
18.	Aldershot	39	46	-12
19.	Wrexham	37	43	-3
20.	Chesterfield	38	44	-10
21.	Maidenhead Utd	38	41	-14
22.	Ebbsfleet Utd	39	42	-21
23.	AFC Fylde	37	39	-16
24.	Chorley	38	26	-34

Chapter 9

Winners and a few losers. 'Thirty years of hurt? Seriously?'

Pandemic-related kick-off times were a mystery. I'm pretty sure I wasn't the only one to have been caught out by my team kicking off at six o'clock but, I suppose, after nearly an entire generation when the staging of matches had little to do with wizened old supporters like me who still trail themselves off to watch games, we should all have been used to it. Into this lucky dip of timings came a further innovation – the 8.15 start.

Presumably this was to accommodate the broadcasting of games at six o'clock, or whatever other arbitrary hour football's paymasters deemed sensible. There was nothing else clogging up the schedules to obstruct them: there are, after all, only so many reruns of top goals from 2007 on a foreshortened screen that even the most lobotomised of sport addicts can tolerate. The other necessary evil of lockdown, the Zoomcast, had run its short course as footballers and pundits engaged in the new national sport of showcasing books that had never been read or displaying newly arranged, tasteful soft furnishings. In defence of the TV companies, another of my personal bugbears, the late finish on a school night, was scarcely relevant for a nation now accustomed to donning pyjamas as its daily mode of dress – and, yes, I get it: there were definitely more things to get irritated about.

By the time Chelsea played Manchester City on the (late) evening of 25 June, we'd begun to come to terms with this new world of TV coverage and here, for the first time, was a game with a real potential sting as an outcome. Liverpool had come out of lockdown and trudged their way through a somnolent, spiritless Merseyside derby, but had steered themselves back on course with a 4-0 dismantling of Palace a few days later. If City failed to win at Stamford Bridge the next day, Liverpool would be champions. Chelsea had ambitions of their own to pursue in terms of gaining a place in the Champions League. Even though they were never going to be champions. And even though the notion that football's authorities might hold fire on this money-spinner to ease fixture congestion in an uncertain future was as likely as a rocking horse producing excrement.

With the score at 1-1 and City looking favourites to win the game, Chelsea broke away and in a scramble on the goal line, Fernandinho did a little bit of juggling to treat us all to another massively entertaining and game-enhancing episode of VAR. Fernandinho sent off, Willian dispatches the penalty, reasonably muted celebrations in the empty cavernousness, but in the homes and streets of the red part of Liverpool the pent-up frustration of all those decades of non-achievement was lanced at last as dancing in the streets commenced.

Goodness knows, those 30 barren years must have been a trial for those loyal, stoical supporters. In all that time, all they had to sustain their faith and enthusiasm for the club they loved were three victories in the FA Cup and four in the various manifestations of the League Cup. There was just the one triumph in the UEFA Cup, and two victories in the top European trophy, one of which – the miracle in Istanbul – was one of the greatest feats in modern football. In 2019 they topped this off with victory in the FIFA World Club Cup, stemming their progress in the League Cup because of the ensuing fixture congestion – so what a waste of time that turned out to be. Quite how those fans managed to endure it all and stay so resolutely humble and cheerful was a mystery to the rest of the football world.

Liverpool manager, Jürgen Klopp, along with a series of official announcements and statements from the club, had pleaded, Canute-like, with fans to celebrate responsibly, which, of course, the majority did. Social media churned out image after image of clumsy dancing and almost-hugs in front gardens, living rooms and socially distanced, gazebo-protected gatherings from across the region. I'll be gracious and avoid comment about how they were also dancing in the streets of Torquay and Kuala Lumpur (see what I did there?). Not everyone, though, was as public-minded and the response from politicians who, if they had possessed even a modicum of self-awareness after the escapades of the PM's chief adviser, should have remined diplomatically silent, was drearily predictable.

The chief executive of the Premier League, Richard Masters, was summonsed to appear before the parliamentary sub-committee for Digital, Culture, Media and Sport to answer as to whether the league accepted 'responsibility for what could well be a very, very nasty spike' in coronavirus cases in the city. You may wish to take a second to read that sentence back to yourself: the parliamentarians who had presided over the worst record of cases and deaths in Europe wanted to know whether the Premier League wanted to accept some accountability for its actions. Leading the charge was Steve Brine, Conservative MP for the footballing metropolis that is Winchester: 'When you've got players in a hotel garden hugging each other, jumping up and down and celebrating with each other, of course the fans were going to do the same.'

It comes to something when the openly Tory-supporting *Telegraph* is the journal that is left to point out some home truths. Its chief sports writer, Paul Hayward, captured a common response in his observation:

> *The Government formed by Steve Brine's party is hardly weighed down with garlands for its handling of the coronavirus crisis or the easing of lockdown restrictions. By consent, the Dominic Cummings fiasco is among the reasons why people in England have run harder and faster with their new semi-freedoms than the Government and its scientists would like.*

Hayward's judgement may well be sound, but he was, of course, swimming against the tide. The behaviour of football fans and, let's not be coy, Liverpool fans in particular, is held to a higher standard by those in high office who rarely understand the game and its place in people's hearts. When the beaches at Bournemouth were clogged, or even when London parks suddenly became the focus of public indignation because of a perceived lack of social distancing, there was no discourse about 'typical Dorset people' or 'bloody city dwellers'. Observers of a sceptical disposition may even be inclined to suggest that the antics of a few drunks on Merseyside, as inexcusable as their actions were, provided a welcome shift of focus for some who had shortcomings of their own to answer for.

There were few who begrudged Liverpool their success, but for neutrals, as far as the top of the Premier League was concerned, it was always going to be a case of what happened after the Lord Mayor's show. There was the diverting spectacle a few days later of Manchester City taking apart a team so obviously hung-over that it wouldn't have been a surprise if they'd had Alka-Seltzer in their drinks-break bottles, but apart from the tussle for places in a European competition that was little more than a mirage on the horizon, it was at the bottom of the table where the real entertainment was to be had.

Nothing, perhaps, captures the bewildering stupidity of the modern game more than the actions of owners for whom football clubs are acquisitions or assets, rather than parts of people's lives, loves, histories and family traditions. Right up there in the roll call of dishonour must be the Pozzo family. The head of this institution is Giampaolo and his son, Gino, is chairman of Watford. During the course of the 2019/20 season, Gino employed three managers, the third of whom, the redoubtable and reliable Nigel Pearson, might just have been the man to dig them out of trouble after the two previous incumbents, Javi Gracia and Quique Sánchez Flores, had amassed a mighty eight points between them from 15 games. In came nuggety Nigel and sorted them out. In a heady period during the depths of winter, he guided Watford to victory against Manchester United, followed by three consecutive wins against Villa, Wolves and Bournemouth. There ensued a rockier time before a truly astonishing victory against Liverpool. In true football style, defeat at Palace followed immediately afterwards, but as lockdown hit, Watford were out of the relegation places, having accrued 19 points from 14 games under Pearson's leadership.

When play resumed, a creditable, dull draw against Leicester was followed by three defeats, but victories against Newcastle and Norwich seemed to lift them out of the mire and, to employ the old chestnut, put their fate in their own hands. What then happened at the so-called London Stadium on 17 July can only be a matter of conjecture and rumour – but what else is football for? Whether Nigel, very properly, thought that the laughable defending that led to a two-goal deficit in the first ten minutes, with a third added before half-time, merited some choice words and teacup smashing, we will never know. The only certainty was that Pearson was sacked, allegedly during the match itself, with two games to go. A Watford-supporting friend was moved to send me a ranting email:

Shock, horror! But for a Watford fan it's perfectly normal behaviour in these abnormal, unsettling lockdown-influenced times. Well, with the ruthless, all-powerful Pozzo family in charge all things are possible. Their brutal remit is if a manager is not successful and his players are not performing, he has to go. But I say: 'Stop the merry-go-round I want to get off.'

And off they did, in fact, go. Right down to the second division as they lost their last two games and Villa were gifted a game against hapless, cup-final bound Arsenal and cruised to a draw at the now safe West Ham. Jack Grealish scored a wonder goal and was immediately made a knight of the realm and Dean Smith and John Terry were carried on the shoulders of their relieved accountants to the rapturous applause of a virtual, digitised Holte End. Who are you calling bitter? Bournemouth accompanied Watford and Norwich to the Championship. They were to be replaced by Leeds, who defied expectations and remained resolutely intact, and West Brom, who survived a few hiccups to hold on to a merited second place. And then there were the play-offs.

The play-off system was introduced into top-level football in England in 1987. The idea was to minimise the number of games towards the end of the season that became meaningless as teams with nothing to play for drifted along aimlessly in a series of pointless games. On a personal level, at least until the late 1990s, this meandering was a virtually unknown experience. As a Birmingham City supporter there was almost always some frantic last-minute scrabbling. Very occasionally this may have been at the top of the table. More often than not it was at the bottom and involved not just your own results but weeks of speculation about the permutations that could possibly mean salvation. Overall, however, the play-offs did the job of maintaining a degree of interest for a longer period for more clubs.

Their first manifestation in 1987 was in a different format from the one with which we are now familiar. The three clubs below the two promoted automatically went into a mini-league with the club just above the relegation places in the division above. This set-up only lasted for two years. The finals were two-legged affairs with games at neutral venues to be played in the event of an overall draw. This happened twice in 1987 and once in 1988, where the Third Division final was played at Walsall's Fellows Park, which would have been fine and dandy if Walsall themselves had not been in it. After a 3-3 aggregate score in the two preceding games, they brushed aside Bristol City 4-0. In 1990, the final was moved to Wembley.

The arrangements for settling league positions as football prepared for coming out of lockdown ended with the decision that play-offs would be used to determine final promotion places in the top six tiers. The first of these to be played out, as touched on in Chapter 5, saw Northampton Town triumph in the League Two final in an empty Wembley on a Monday afternoon. Whatever manager Keith Curle's men were doing while isolating must have done them some good. Prior to lockdown, they had acquired six points from seven games and slipped to seventh place in the table – and so one of the contested peculiarities of the play-offs, whereby seventh place trumps fourth for success, raised its head again. Not that this bothered the club in any way. Within a few days, its website urged supporters to renew their season tickets without delay. In a detailed explanation of how to do so, there was no recognition of the fact they'd be very lucky to be going down to the Sixfields Stadium in any foreseeable future.

Whatever was in the air in Middle England during the pandemic seemed to be breeding footballing success. The imposing location of the Cobblers' victory was occupied a few days later by Oxford United and Wycombe Wanderers, with the latter winning 2-1 and finding themselves in the second tier of English football for the first time in their history. The club had been in the Football League for fewer than 30 years and like

Burnley and Swansea, who feature in earlier chapters, had faced a last-day elimination in 2014. From a neutral point of view – or maybe this is just me – the principal regret was that the formidable Adebayo Akinfenwa, he of some 600 league appearances in 16 years and the man whose imposing physical presence gives heart to all of us who know it'd be good to shed a pound or two, failed to score after coming on in the 62nd minute.

There was inevitable focus on Wycombe manager, Gareth Ainsworth. With his flowing locks, he pursues his love of music by performing as lead singer with the Cold Blooded Hearts. The band's Facebook page reveals that they were looking for a drummer prior to the final, but there was no immediate indication as to whether Ainsworth's success at Wembley had prompted any enquiries. He had instructed his players and staff to make a different sort of noise of their own during the game to encourage their colleagues. 'My boys were willing to shout and sing, and they didn't care what they looked like. That's what we are. We don't care what we look like if that's what it takes to get the job done.' It was rumoured that a justifiably emotional Ainsworth didn't manage to fulfil all his media commitments the following morning.

By the time the Wycombe manager had recovered his composure, the clubs that were hoping to escape through the top hatch of the Championship which his team had just entered were gearing up for business. The extraordinary story of how Swansea slipped into contention via last-second goals at two venues has been told in Chapter 4. As a consequence, there existed the possibility of an all Welsh or all London final, or any combination thereof. But it was Brentford and Fulham – fittingly the sides who had finished third and fourth respectively – who went off to play in what has now, very tiresomely, been universally dubbed as the most valuable game in football. Not promotion to the highest division; not just reward for planning and careful management (especially so in the case of Brentford); not terrific excitement for the die-hard fans of those clubs. Nope. Promotion meant the gateway to riches and everlasting TV revenue. Maybe. Who knew in a post-pandemic world?

In a final in which the players adhered to what must have been firm instructions not to cross the ball into the box or have a shot at goal, the first 90 minutes were played out against the now familiar background of crowdies but not, mercifully, canned noise. As legs and brains tired in extra time, two pieces of brilliance from full-back Joe Bryan won the game for Fulham. So excited was his manager, Scott Parker, that he lost his tie clip. Brentford had beaten their opponents twice in the regular season but their failure to do so in the richest game in the world (sigh) meant that they would be starting next season in the Championship in the romantically named Brentford Community Stadium which, one imagines, does not have a pub on each corner like dear old Griffin Park. It was their ninth play-off failure – a record – and so their surprising post-lockdown defeats at the hands of Stoke and Barnsley had cost them very dear.

In glorious isolation in the stands, Villa manager Dean Smith had been afforded a pass to watch the Brentford team he had once led. He'd done better than footballing royalty Greg Dyke, once chairman of the club, who had been on the radio in the morning bemoaning the fact that he had not been similarly privileged. Both Smith and Dyke would, no doubt, have been gutted in the regulation way by the outcome, as were contributors on the Beesotted website and Twitter feed. Most conceded that their team had been outplayed on the night, but with the dogged persistence of the one-eyed fan John97931482 insisted that 'Fulham could/ should have had 2 if not 3 red cards. And with VAR they would have done and a penalty.' Like all of us, he probably just needed to get out more.

A few days before the dapper Scott Parker cavorted round an eerie Wembley, we had that much-loved, nation-stopping institution, the FA Cup Final. Plenty has been written and spoken about the demise of the FA Cup, but it does still appear to be a trophy worth winning. In the quarter of a century since Everton won it in 1995, only Portsmouth (2008) and Wigan (2013) have gatecrashed the cabal of both Manchester clubs, Liverpool, Arsenal and Chelsea. Despite the enduring successes of this prestigious group, it was possibly only supporters of clubs who had reached the last eight prior to lockdown who were taking much interest in 2020. And then there they were again, after a set of quarter-final games that seemed to slip by unnoticed, the big boys – two Manchesters, Arsenal and Chelsea in the semi-finals which the FA insisted on staging at an empty Wembley. The two London clubs made it through to the final to be played on the first day of August. If this might have constituted a tiring extension to an already enervating season, the participants were, at least, in a better position than their female counterparts.

By the end of May, the FA Women's Super League was curtailed, and positions decided on a points-per-game basis. Chelsea were declared champions with Aston Villa winning the second division. There was to be no promotion or relegation in tiers two–seven of the women's game. The Women's FA Cup, however, was not abandoned. Having reached the quarter-final stage, Kelly Simmons, the FA director of the women's professional game, announced on 24 July that she was delighted to have received approval for the conclusion. 'The Women's FA Cup is a showpiece fixture in the football calendar and because of that there was huge appetite for the three remaining rounds to be played.' Games were to begin in late September with the final scheduled for 31 October. No one, of course, knew if crowds were to be admitted.

On the eve of the English men's cup final, there had actually been a game of football played in the UK in front of a crowd – well, almost. On Friday, 31 July, a late Robbie McDaid goal brought victory for Glentoran against Ballymena United in the Irish Cup Final – or, to give it its full name, the Sadler's Peaky Blinder Irish Cup Final – in front of 500 fans in Belfast's Windsor Park. 250 supporters from each side had been granted admittance and had engaged in a sing-off prior to kick-off. The internet does not provide ocular proof of this choral event so there is no way of knowing whether it had the effect of inspiring either team. The official capacity of Windsor Park is just over 18,000, so the notion of peas in a drum seems most likely to describe this brave effort.

Had the final been played in England, even these 500 privileged souls would have been unable to attend. On that same Friday, the English government withdrew permission for the pilot events where crowds could be admitted on a limited basis. A day earlier, a tightening of restrictions in the Greater Manchester area had been imposed at startlingly short notice as a response to an increase in infections. The Prime Minister then spoke of 'squeezing the brake pedal' on the easing of lockdown, a position reinforced by the chief medical officer, Chris Whitty, warning that we had 'probably reached the near limit of what we can do' in terms of easing up if the nation was to be in a position to get all children back into school by September – a critical factor in kick-starting a spluttering economy. At that point the number of deaths related to Covid-19 in the UK was 46,119 – 41,082 of which had been in England.

We tried to forget that for a moment as at teatime on 1 August, Arsenal came from behind to beat Chelsea. I half-watched it in a socially distanced way in a sunny pub garden, accompanied by a fair number of supporters of both sides. I live just north of London in leafy St Albans and so, in some ways, it is unsurprising that those with such affiliations should be resident there. This has not always been the norm. Some 30 years ago I taught at a comprehensive school in the city where, broadly speaking, most of the support was divided between Watford and Luton. It is a mark of a changing demographic, along with the unrelenting marketisation of the game, that although there is still ample evidence of residual loyalty to these local teams, their replica shirts in parks and pubs are now relatively rare. Anyway, to the low-key joy of those in red, too many of whom regard success as some sort of footballing birth right, the cup was lifted – well, dropped actually – by Arsenal captain Pierre-Emerick Aubameyang and their supporters gleefully began thinking about booking those attractive Thursday night trips in the Europa League.

The day afterwards at the same venue, Harrogate Town won promotion to the Football League. It was a remarkable achievement for a club that had only been in the fifth tier of English football for a couple of years and for their manager since 2009, Simon Weaver. At 42 years of age, that meant that he had spent a quarter of his life managing the team, now owned by his dad. For Notts County, one of the oldest clubs in the country and the one that has undergone more relegations than anyone else, it marked the end of a miserable few days for the city, following Forest's cataclysmic collapse in failing to reach the play-offs. Not, of course, that there would have been any mutual losing of love. One of English football's lesser known quirks is the fact that County open up their social club to supporters going to see their team away at Forest (and very pleasant it is too), thereby ensuring that they happily profit when their neighbours are in town.

You had to hope that Harrogate had a clear idea of what they were letting themselves in for. With only one team relegated from League Two, they, along with Barrow, looked like they'd be replacing Stevenage, who only found themselves in bottom place because

Macclesfield had escaped with a surprisingly light two-point penalty for the non-payment of wages. The club issued a statement on 20 June in which they said that they 'would like to express our gratitude to the independent arbitration panel for their unquestionable diligence, in reaching what we deem to be a fair and unbiased conclusion'. Well, yes, you might well say that, wouldn't you? Except that ten days later, in the sort of muddled timing and communication that has become the hallmark of how the EFL deals with rule-breakers, the suspended four-point penalty was applied with immediate effect and down they went – some four weeks before the new season was due to start. (I can't keep doing late edits, but there's every chance that things will have changed by the time you're reading this.)

Harrogate would also be in the same division as hapless Bolton, who had been playing in the Premier League only nine years previously. Up in the Championship, or possibly League One, Charlton and Wigan were making bellicose noises about legal challenges to the EFL's decision to dock 12 points from Sheffield Wednesday at the start of the new season as opposed to the current one – making a difference to their own relegations. Derby County – and goodness knew who else – sat shivering in the wings. Meanwhile, supporters of AFC Bury would have noted with pleasure that on 21 July, an official announcement on the website of the North West Counties Football League confirmed the club's admittance.

In the meantime, winners or losers, we all stuck our fingers in our ears as the news of more localised spikes in Covid infection wormed their way into the headlines. But through it all, football had, somehow, managed to bring its competitive business for 2019/20 to some sort of conclusion.

Chapter 10

And how was it for you? Well, pretty dreadful as you're asking

This is nothing more than a brief personal footnote – albeit a pretty disastrous one in footballing terms. It does, though, tell the story of the team that turned out to have the fifth worst post-lockdown record in Europe – the 'winners' of that dismal title being Norwich City, in case you're interested.

I had my say in full about what it's like to be a Birmingham City supporter in my earlier book, *Hugging Strangers*, so readers will be spared all the gory details. Nevertheless, as far as my relationship with the club is concerned, the weeks after restart were shocking, even by the high standards we have set ourselves over the decades.

At the beginning of April, shortly after football finished, an old school friend emailed me. Like me, his first visit to St Andrew's was in 1963. Life and work had intervened and it was not until I started going back to watch football on a regular basis in the mid-1990s, once my days of hacking and lumbering round parks' pitches had mercifully come to an end, that we would see each other at games and resume our active friendship. Also like me, and I relate this not out of any sense of boastfulness, he has enjoyed a successful professional career, raising a family along the way, is well travelled and is now enjoying the joys of semi-retirement. This is all by way of background before asking the perennially puzzling question. Why would two such relatively accomplished individuals allow their mood and outlook on life to be altered, however temporarily, by the actions of a group of young men with whom they would have little in common, but who just happened to be wearing a version of a football shirt that was part of their personal history? I don't know the answer: I'm just putting it up for debate.

Anyway, this is what he wrote:

On a positive – and entirely serious – note (well, I leave you to judge), I can report that my anxiety levels and mental health in general have improved dramatically in recent weeks, thanks to the lack of football and thus the absence of any need to think about BCFC and its shortcomings …

The world was facing a threat that still, at the time of writing, is barely understood. Supermarket shelves were beginning to look ominously empty. The country's Prime Minister was about to be taken into intensive care ... and the mental health of my highly accomplished, intelligent friend was improving because he was being spared his annual frustration at his team's insistence on its usual flirtation with disaster. Don't get me wrong. I'm not condemning him in any way: I know exactly how he felt and shared his relief.

We should have revelled even more in this anxiety-free space because once football resumed, Birmingham City surpassed themselves in utter incompetence as they pursued their quest for failure with greater vigour than ever.

When my friend wrote to me, the Blues were sitting in relative comfort in 16th place in the Championship with 47 points from 37 games, eight points above the drop zone. History would suggest that another five or six points from the remaining nine games would be more than enough to avoid any chance of relegation. Old-timers like my friend and I knew much better than to apply anything like logic to such a situation. We'd been here before – and straightaway we could begin to smell something unpleasant.

Before a ball had been kicked, the club announced that Pep Clotet would be leaving once the season had been played out. You may have noticed that I didn't call him the manager and that's because when he ceased to be the assistant to Garry Monk, who had left in July 2019, the club's owners thought it a good idea to bestow on him the title of caretaker head coach. How wanted and secure that must have made him feel although, to be fair, with a CV that was – let's be kind – varied and indifferent, there was an argument to say he was already punching way above his weight. When he took over, he was the club's fifth whatever-he-was in just over two and a half years. Along the way, the owners had sacked two bright sparks in Monk and Gary Rowett and allowed Harry Redknapp five months of reckless spending before realising quite what they'd done. Gianfranco Zola and Steve Cotterill are best left to rest quietly in the dusty corners of the club's history.

Once the streaming services allowed us a glimpse of Pep Clotet, he looked like what he must have been: an unhappy man waiting impatiently to get home. Prior to lockdown, his wife and two children had returned to the family home in Igualada, near Barcelona. In this, if not in his footballing acumen, he showed foresight and wisdom. 'We know what is coming,' he told the *Birmingham Mail*. 'But I don't think people in England do.' There were 2,000 cases a week in Spain at the time; if the UK government was putting its fingers in its ears and hoping, Pep was not and, what's more, he was able to give us a glimpse into our unimagined future: 'In Spain right now people do not go into the streets, except to buy groceries. You cannot even go out to exercise. It is like a scene from *The Walking Dead*!'

Whether it was an understandable preoccupation with his distant family or a misguided feeling that it was just a case of playing out a few games, picking up the odd point here and there, we'll never know. As it happens, the immediate return was not too discouraging. A park-the-bus draw at league leaders West Brom and a sloppy 3-3 mess at home to struggling Hull took us to 49 from 39. Still OK, you'd think.

There then followed a sequence of results and performances of utter, miserable ineptitude. Four straight defeats and just one goal scored. After the third of these, at home to Swansea, social media was awash with stories that Pep Clotet had failed to appear at the regulation post-match conference. A spokesperson for the club informed us that 'he had somewhere else to be'. Unsurprisingly, that somewhere else turned out to be Spain.

A formal statement the next day churned out the old 'mutual consent' nonsense and a former player and youth coach took over. Three games to go – three points and we'd definitely be OK. Another hapless defeat took the club nearer to the drop and only a very late equaliser against fellow strugglers Charlton – who were eventually relegated – stemmed the flow of defeats. It didn't quite do the job of ensuring safety and so, for the fourth time in seven years, the team that bears the name of the second city went into the last day of the season fighting to survive the drop to the third level of English football.

The club has a proud – if that's the correct term – record of pulling stunning performances out of the bag in such circumstances. This time was different. In a home game against Derby, we were a goal down after five minutes and lost 3-1, gifting them goals of mind-boggling stupidity. Elsewhere, newly anointed champions, Leeds, did us a favour by beating Charlton and we stayed up. I can rarely remember feeling less elated at such an anti-climactic, passive way to cling to safety.

If tin lids needed putting on a dreadful end to the season, the sparkling talent that is Jude Bellingham departed, as we all knew he would, with Borussia Dortmund acquiring his services. There was never any doubt that he would have to leave. The fee was reported as £26m, which, one hoped, would go some way to meeting the club's enduring financial shortfalls. It is a measure of how expectations among supporters now slither in the bottom of the swamp that nobody trusted the club's owners to use this windfall wisely. In an embarrassing move, the club 'retired' Bellingham's number 22 shirt. He'd played for us on fewer than 50 occasions and scored four goals. Meanwhile, down the Soho Road, Albion got promoted and over the expressway the Villa somehow eluded relegation. So, with all our principal neighbours and rivals lording it up with the elite, there we were again in nondescript limbo making daft gestures that looked small-time.

I have had a standing joke with my wife and partner of over 40 years. A couple of years after I went back to watching football regularly, I bought a season ticket, even though home games necessitated a 200-mile round trip. Although Birmingham City have enjoyed the occasional holiday in the Premier League since then, making it a worthwhile purchase, for much of the time it has merely allowed me enjoyable days out, spoilt only by having to watch the Blues. In a silly family ritual, I'll come home from games disappointed and dutifully say, 'Right. That's it. I'm not renewing that bloody season ticket next year.' My wife's equally ritualistic response is to say, 'I'm going to have that inscribed on your gravestone.'

By mid-July 2020, with Birmingham City hanging on by fingertips to second division survival, the club was not yet in a position to inform fans about the procedures for season-ticket renewal. As the country grappled with whether or not we were supposed to be wearing a face mask, allowed to go to gyms and, much more importantly, how we were going to get back to work, school and college, I boldly made my own life-changing decision. I'd wait and see what happened before I renewed.

A final couple of footnotes to this admittedly self-indulgent chapter. The first is that watching football during this period was the polar opposite of everything I enjoy about being a supporter. From conversations with other addicts, I know that my reaction was far from unique. By definition, I was almost always on my own and although constant texting and messaging supplied some sort of communication – usually to share the misery around a bit – no one could possibly pretend that it was compensation for the communal experience of going to a game. A quiet, bottled pint sitting on the sofa is not the sort of pre-match ritual that anyone needs in their life. The inane commentary of the club's streaming service, a combination of baffling tactical explanations and the dronings of the bloke who usually sits behind you, was worse than, well … the bloke who sits behind you. (To be entirely fair, he can be marginally entertaining on occasions.) It was a sort of football, but not as we knew it or wanted it to be.

The second is this – and if it speaks ill of me, then at least I know I'm not on my own. In the days following Birmingham City's post-lockdown run of three draws and six defeats which took us to the brink of relegation, there were any number of genuinely alarming things happening in the real world. As far as anyone could trust the numbers, deaths from Covid-19 in the UK surpassed 45,000; serious economic forecasters warned of an unemployment rate of 11.7 per cent; China made disconcerting noises about the UK government's rejection of Huawei and, in a move that could only have been the result of a drinking dare in Downing Street, Chris Grayling was appointed head of the national Intelligence and Security Committee (although this appointment was rescinded fairly sharply). Against this background, when trusty Lukas Jutkiewicz bundled the ball over the line for an injury-time equaliser against Charlton Athletic to temporarily ease our relegation fears, the world, just for a few moments and in one household, seemed a better place.

Make of that what you will.

Chapter 11

Southern League. Royston Town stopped in their tracks with success in their sights

Other than taking on the job of treasurer, Alan Barton has done just about everything that one person could possibly do for a football club. He started playing for Royston Town in 1975 in the Hertfordshire County Premier League and was elected president in 1996. He's one of the trustees of the club and has played a leading role in developing its activities on and off the field of play. To top it all off, he spent four years lovingly putting together the story of the club since its inception in 1875 in a 350-page volume. To leaf through it is to gain an insight into some social, as well as football, history as Alan charts the involvement of local people in maintaining and building a community amenity that has its roots in a time when, if it wasn't exactly jumpers for goalposts, the local paper could report on how a game against neighbours Saffron Walden was settled by a disputed decision about whether the tape between the goalposts 'had been the proper height (8 feet), it being only 6 feet'.

That local paper glories in the marvellous name of *The Royston Crow* and was founded in 1855 by John Warren. It takes its name from the bird which adorns the town's crest and it is also how the football club is referred to by everyone. The town of Royston, with its 15,000 population, sits in the north of Hertfordshire close to the border with Cambridgeshire. Like many places in the region, its agricultural roots, although still evident, no longer define the town. According to the last full UK census, half of the population fit into the top social grade and occupation categories, unemployment is well below the national average and home ownership, at 63 per cent, is nearly four times higher than that of social and council housing. The town has a self-contained feel and the club's ground at Garden Walk, itself testament to the tenacity and energy of people like Alan in their determination to develop it, sits neatly on its eastern edge, very much part of the landscape.

For anyone acquainted with the game at this level, Alan's book will mirror their experience. Dotted with images of everything from stalwarts from its history to those pre-war team photos where every player looks as though he's 45 if he's a day, it's all there. Before and after photos of the new clubhouse – 'the chairman adds a finishing touch with the paint pot' – to the charity match featuring Martin Peters and Dennis Waterman. We've got the friendly against Spurs in 1985, Glenn Hoddle and all, and, of course, that celebrated 22-man brawl against Stony Stratford in 2008. To be fair, Alan downplays the incident. Although *The Crow* headline shrieked, 'Police called after match brawl', Alan's view is that 'things were always under control and the headline was, like many, a bit over-dramatic'. As a window into football at this semi-professional level, it's a charming way to while away a couple of lockdown afternoons.

Threaded throughout the book is the story of a club which, despite the usual flirtations with failure and stuttering progress has, in recent years, climbed steadily through the leagues to sit now in the Southern League Premier Division Central – effectively the seventh tier of English football. The Crows played their last league game before lockdown in front of 415 people at Garden Walk and handed out a 5-0 drubbing to St Ives (Cambridgeshire, not Cornwall) which left them in third position with 63 points from 30 games. Ahead of them were Tamworth with 65 from 30, and topping the league were Peterborough Sports, who had played three games more than both of their closest rivals. It wasn't quite the Crows' last game. On the following

Tuesday, only 83 people turned up to witness a similar 5-0 thumping of Hemel Hempstead in the semi-final of the Herts FA Charity Cup – a worthy, but not prestigious, competition – and that was that. The FA reached a swift decision on 26 March, stating that it had 'reached a consensus that the 2019/20 season will now be brought to an end, and all results will be expunged. This will mean no promotion or relegation of clubs.' The third oldest football club in Hertfordshire was now consigned to doing what the whole nation was doing in a range of different contexts: waiting and seeing.

I speak to Alan on a gloomy July afternoon and when I mention how frustrating it must have been for the club to have had the plug pulled when things were going so well, he sighs with regret and exasperation. The players, he tells me, were utterly convinced that they were going to win the league. A successful run in the FA Trophy had been instrumental in amplifying this belief, not least because of a stunning victory over Hertfordshire's third-most senior club after Stevenage and Watford, Boreham Wood, just prior to Christmas. Eventually, defeat to Concord Rangers in the quarter-final just before lockdown put that particular dream on hold and the Trophy competition was suspended. All the same, Alan waxes lyrical about one of the biggest days of their season. 'If you could have seen it. All the kids running on, the players in the bar afterwards. It's exactly what football at this level is about.' When the season was truncated it was 'like going into mourning'.

Lockdown hit Royston Town with a vengeance. With crowds levelling out at around the 400 mark – something like a tenfold increase from ten years previously – the loss of revenue hit hard. Entrance charges of £10 and £6 were lost, as were bar takings, money from the 50/50 draw, raffles and, of course, the letting of the clubhouse for functions. The annual music and beer festival, attracting around 1,500 people to see local bands and enjoy the profits made from beer supplied by the Greene King brewery, was another huge blow. Alan is properly discreet when I ask him about payments to players but reveals that the two top earners are 'in the region' of £400 per week, with most of the others on a 'lot, lot less'. I feel it best not to push him about retainers, but the basic picture is one that is in sharp focus – this is a club, like hundreds of others at this level, that has had its financial throat cut.

Although, not quite. A crowdfunding appeal intended to address the estimated shortfall of some £50,000 – Keep the Crows Flying – has raised half of that amount much more quickly than anyone anticipated. 'We were wary of asking for money at times like this,' Alan explains, 'but people were wonderful – a couple of quid here, a fiver there. It showed us how much the club meant to the town.' Players have worked hard to involve themselves in the community and this has clearly paid off. The basic ambition of everyone involved with the Crows, to ensure that there would be a football club in existence at the end of it all, seems to have been rewarded.

We chat about a future shrouded in mystery. The basic core of players has just started individual training and tentative agreement about their terms has been reached. As to when any future season may start and how long it will last and under what conditions it will be played, we're in guessing territory. How will the unknown work patterns of part-timers fit with whatever does emerge? It's bad enough, he tells me, for players to negotiate time off work in order to play during the week in relatively settled times and he finishes our chat with a story that epitomises life below the glamour lines.

An evening game against Bromsgrove on a filthy evening – 120 miles, two and a half hours. A phone call before they set off to ensure that the game will be on – and off they go. With depressing inevitability, they arrive at the ground to news of the dreaded pitch inspection and the equally foreseeable announcement of the game being off. So, everybody back on the coach? Not so fast. The driver's rest time dictates that they can't set off until the scheduled end of the game. They hang around in the clubhouse, get home at 1 in the morning and some set off to work at 6, all without a ball having been kicked. You've got to love the game to be part of something like that.

When it comes to loving the game, manager Steve Castle is up there with the best. With nearly 500 appearances in the Football League and another 60 or so in the semi-professional divisions, Steve has been manager of Royston since 2013. Over 250 of his appearances were for Leyton Orient, close to his place of birth, although his family affiliations – 'my old man was Hackney through and through' – are with Tottenham Hotspur. During our conversation we veer towards comparison between football at that elevated level and the more modest surroundings in which he now plies his trade. He'd quite like to take his two teenage sons to see Spurs but his own commitments and the price differential are significant factors in preventing this from happening. When we talk about the possibility of lower-league clubs attracting greater numbers once post-lockdown football gets going in the new, as yet unimagined season, he would like to think that would happen, but, like all of us, is sure of nothing. 'It'd save me a few quid,' he tells me. 'We can all go down to watch Bishops Stortford (his local club), have a hot dog each and I'm still only about 25 quid down. I can't do that at Tottenham and I'm better off than many.' Above all, though, Steve believes that football at its highest, commercial level does not, and cannot, involve individuals in their club and community in the way that attachment to Royston Town can provide.

'I'm really proud of what we've got here. It's got a really special place in my heart.' He's had offers to operate at a higher level but feels that his connection to the Crows and community, along with firm support from the club's chairman, would render any such move foolhardy. Not that he's dewy-eyed about how football works. 'The results have been the main thing in terms of getting these bigger crowds. It hasn't always been like this – but you cash in on the good times.' In terms of pride, he makes particular mention of players from the club who have progressed to the Football League and sees this as testament to a club that looks after people, nurtures their talent and encourages proper conduct on and off the field of play.

We talk at a time when the post-Covid Premier League is just about to draw to a close. As an ex-pro, Steve has not been impressed by what he's seen. 'I've never played at the very top,' he explains (he got as high as the Championship) 'but I've got to be honest. I know everyone seemed to want it back, but what we've had is a watered-down version of the game.' When we consider why this might be, we mull over a few thoughts. The most obvious is that the absence of crowds has contributed to the dullness. There must have been a lack of match sharpness in the early games, many of which were notable for players making inexplicable, elementary errors, but Steve suggests there was probably a tendency on the part of some observers to forget that everyone involved in the game, including the players, had been through the same psychological and emotional mill that society as a whole had experienced. 'Pep Guardiola lost his mum to the virus and right across the country players' mindset will have been affected if they've suffered a loss.' It's a telling comment from someone whose view of football being about human beings and not just results or money informs everything he says.

When it comes to the future, however, Steve slips into understandable manager mode. As far as Royston Town is concerned, there is unfinished business. He is convinced that they were well placed to win the league and that this remains the obvious ambition for the new season. As it happens, a couple of days after we speak, media reports began to talk of a general return to the game at all levels from mid-September. A visit to the website of the FA revealed ... absolutely nothing. This would have come as no surprise to Steve who has been unimpressed by the quality of communication from the game's authorities. All the same, measures are being put in pace for the possibility of competitive friendlies in August with a view to continue building on their success once the season starts. I tell him that I'm genuinely looking forward to getting to a Crows game as soon as

I can and, like Alan Barlow, he promises to buy me a pint when I do. We part on Zoom, hoping to meet one day in real life.

It's a story of the times.

Southern League Premier Division
Royston Town stymied on the brink of success. (Redditch United supporters – look away now.)

Final position		Played	Points	GD
1.	Peterborough Sports	33	65	44
2.	Tamworth	30	65	66
3.	Royston Town	30	63	34
4.	Bromsgrove Sporting	32	57	37
5.	Rushall Olympic	33	53	15
6.	Stourbridge	32	53	1
7.	Banbury Utd	32	52	17
8.	Coalville Town	30	51	19
9.	Nuneaton Borough	33	50	11
10.	Kings Langley	30	50	10
11.	Rushden and Diamonds	30	49	5
12.	Barwell	32	48	4
13.	Needham Market	33	48	3
14.	Hednesford Town	32	47	6
15.	Biggleswade Town	30	43	-1
16.	Lowestoft Town	33	41	-14
17.	Hitchin Town	32	39	-6
18.	Stratford Town	33	28	-32
19.	Leiston	32	26	-48
20.	St Ives Town	33	23	-43
21.	Alvechurch	30	17	-33
22.	Redditch United	33	12	-65

Chapter 12

Grassroots football. Working for diversity and inclusivity as we approach the new normal

When lockdown started, those of us who were able to do so went for a daily walk, run or cycle. Amidst all the confusion and mixed messages slopped out from the government briefings, this was the one element that was clear: you could go out and exercise for half an hour. It turned out that doing so had a slightly anarchic, liberated feel as we walked in the middle of traffic-free roads and started noticing things like birdsong and stuff growing. It wasn't all sunshine and roses, though.

First there were the intimate joggers who snuck up on you with their panting and microbe splashing and who clearly weren't graduates from the Cummings School of Social Distancing. Yet, as irritating as that was, it was something else that captured the dispiriting nature of the times: the tapes and locks on the children's playgrounds making them inaccessible territory. There was the odd parent and child bravely bumping a football back and forth to each other outside the fence, but the roistering, yelping games of three-a-side in the fixed, metal nets were notable only for their silent absence. Only after the Prime Minister's bewildering speech on the evening of Sunday, 10 May did we eventually begin to see small groups gathering to kick around at a suitable distance. Shortly afterwards, it became more common to see a few kids with cones, bibs and admirable volunteers doing their drills at a distance. For the kids themselves, in their inevitable branded tops, this was the beginning of the return to football. Their older, playing siblings would have longer to wait.

The game at grassroots level has undergone significant changes in the past two decades. For many men of a certain generation – and I'm being gender-specific for the moment – adult football took place within a timeworn framework. Once you'd left school or full-time education, where teams to play for were part of the make-up of that institution, a work colleague or a friend of a friend would tell you about the Saturday or Sunday team they played for and would you like to come along – and that was pretty well that. You knew what you were signing up for. Meet outside pub, church or school; grumble while you waited for the recidivist latecomers; change together in cramped, liniment-infused cells; go out and play on pitches of varying gradients and misshapenness, refereed by a bloke who made the centre circle his own; scrabble around in your pockets for your match fee; shower together in white-tiled, concrete luxury and then go for a pint.

Even before Covid struck, that was no longer the model. A walk through your local playing fields on a Saturday afternoon or Sunday morning, where back-to-back games once filled every available pitch, became a much quieter excursion. But drive past your local sports centre on any given evening and note the smaller, floodlit pitches occupied to capacity. Work patterns and changes in social habits may have made the traditional Saturday or Sunday game less popular – although by no means, as we shall see, consigned to history – but the desire to play the game at whatever level and, tellingly, no matter your gender or age, remains unchanged.

According to the FA survey into adults' participation in grassroots football conducted in July 2019, over eight million people over the age of 18 were playing the game in 'any format and for any frequency'. In a separate report, the FA was able to claim that there were 1,250 centres where girls between the ages of five and 11 could play. The organisation's Participation Tracker revealed that 2.6 million girls and women played football in 2019. On top of that, there were over 1,000 walking football clubs. The organisation Age UK's study of these came to the unsurprising conclusion that walking football led to 'improvements in physical and mental health and well-being'. I'm all in favour of meticulous, illuminating research, but I'm bound to observe, 'Who knew?'

For all these different ways of playing the game, old-fashioned 11-a-side football remains the favoured form for a significant, if decreasing, number of people. The FA participation survey makes the bold assertion that '11-a-side footballers report higher levels of health and happiness compared to other types of football' – this despite the average of £326 per year that it costs them to play. Given that the FA itself admits that one in three pitches for grassroots use is inadequate, notwithstanding the growing use of artificial surfaces, sticking with parks football is obviously a treasured way of life for many.

It certainly is for Darrion Davis. He's currently the manager of Northumberland Park Rangers who play in the Barnet Sunday Premier League and whose home ground is on the public playing fields at Bullsmore Lane in Enfield. Darrion is quick to admit that 'manager' is a rather grand title for someone who does all the club's paperwork, kit care and general dogsbodying, although the upshot of all of that is he does get to take charge of training every Tuesday and is convinced that his methods are bearing fruit. It's difficult to tell because the website of the league has expunged all results for the 2019/20 season, entering 'void' as the outcome. Rangers's last recorded result is a 3-7 defeat at the hands of Continental FC in the Senior Cup.

Continental were also the club's opponents in the final league game prior to lockdown on 15 March. By this time many players were already reluctant to venture out to play, leaving Darrion with only nine established members of the club to endure the dreaded double-header. For those unfamiliar with the device, this is a way of squeezing in two games on one day to enable all fixtures to be fulfilled – which is something of an irony, given that this was the last scheduled fixture to feature on the league's website, complete with a V for 'void' where the result should be. It's probably just as well: Northumberland Park came out worse on both occasions, 1-3 and 0-7. A few days later, all clubs in the league received an email informing them that the entire season was null and void. The printed league table appears as a series of zeros in every column with Northumberland Park sitting in sixth out of eight places, based on alphabetical order. When I ask Darrion whether he was satisfied with how information was communicated from the league, he shrugs. It was nothing more than a reflection from the very top, he suggests, going on to make me laugh by asking, 'If Boris Johnson was in your circle of friends, would you take advice from him?'

The club is looking for players for the coming season, as are Continental, who proudly claim on their website to be 'a predominantly black team, which was founded in 1958 and makes us one of, if not the oldest black club in Britain'. I talk to Darrion about the ethnic composition of Northumberland Park and he tells me about there being a definite core of black players as well as young men from Brazil, Portugal, the Democratic Republic of Congo and pretty well anywhere in the world. 'We've even got a Romanian goalkeeper,' he tells me, and although I fail to see why this merits specific comment, I don't push him on it. He tells me that although the upsurge in interest in the Black Lives Matter movement took place after lockdown, racism has always been a fact of life in football at this level.

Northumberland Park Rangers take their name from their Tuesday night training location, close to what was White Hart Lane and is now called something that nobody really knows. When Darrion first became involved, the club was playing under the auspices of the Hertfordshire FA, taking them some distance north of the city into areas with fewer black people. Not that there wasn't plenty of home-grown racism of their own to confront. Darrion had taken over from 'George, an old bloke, about 75 years old and a proper old-school racist. Not his fault,' he explains charitably, 'it was just about his age and being East End born and bred.'

He goes on to furnish me with a selection of some of George's choicest comments, with which I am not going to sully these pages. Up in Hertfordshire – although probably nowhere near as remote as arctic Royston – Darrion felt that lack of familiarity with young black men and their conduct was often construed by referees and locals alike as threatening. Eventually the decision was made to relocate to a league closer to home, which made sense geographically with opponents based within easier reach. Not that the move further south has been without its challenging moments.

Darrion tells me of a lively disagreement at the League's AGM in which he challenged one of the leading committee members, accusing him of using racial stereotypes when it came to assessing a case brought against Northumberland Park. He readily accepts that the club had acquired a reputation over the years for 'fighting and arguing' but was adamant that the worst offenders had been weeded out. The incident in question resulted in the club being charged by the London FA with 'failing to control its players': Darrion is adamant that there were extenuating circumstances. Those of us familiar with football on the parks will recognise the situation immediately.

For football at this level to take place, a referee is required. When these rhino-skinned heroes turn up, everyone breathes a sigh of relief – the game can go ahead. Linesmen? Don't be daft. Flags are thrust into the mitts of those too slow and stupid to make themselves scarce and they're lumbered. Which is just about OK if the poor unfortunate is stationed on the side of the pitch occupied by his gang of camp followers. In the remote loneliness of the far touchline, it's a different story. Which is where the Northumberland Park institution known by the players as either Elder or Uncle found himself plying his trade and, unavoidably, incurring the wrath of the opposition. A dodgy decision, an exchange of words and soon the 45-year-old is in a headlock, prompting a mass brawl and the abandonment of the game. Northumberland's opponents are awarded the game and progress to the next round of the cup competition; Darrion's team face the wrath of the FA.

Darrion is convinced first that the incident was provoked by racially charged comments and that the local FA and its committee are not affording his team a fair hearing. He contacts the organisation Kick It Out to make them aware of what has happened and of the extenuating circumstances of the attack on Uncle. However influential or otherwise these actions may have been, he feels exonerated by the fact the charge is dropped with the club merely incurring an administration fee. For Darrion, that is all in the past.

For the season that is to come, whatever form it may take, preparations are already in place. They're hoping for a September start. Public liability and personal injury insurance have been put in place for the players. Affiliation fees have been paid and pitches have notionally been booked. The club knows that it needs to improve its public face and so is looking to improve its presence on Twitter and Instagram. Tuesday night training has started – 'it's a job to get them to do drills, they just want to play' – and the recruitment drive continues apace. For Darrion, this is a chance to rebuild. By day he is a housing support officer, dealing with young people in difficult circumstances. His strong sense of duty and commitment to the welfare of these young people informs everything he does for Northumberland Park. He's working hard to bring 'young black guys with good jobs' into the club to act as 'role models and build the club as a community'. When we finish our digital conversation in early July, I tell him that I am genuinely looking forward to meeting him and his players at the first opportunity; I think it's fair to say that we part on a note of cautious optimism.

While Northumberland Park, Continental and other largely black teams continue to work hard to make grassroots football the location for inclusivity and fighting prejudice, another battle continues to be waged. In 2017, Rory Magrath, an academic from Solent University, published some research about homophobic chanting at football matches. There is little doubt that the team which finds itself most often at the centre of this juvenile, outdated nonsense is Brighton and Hove Albion. Estimates vary, but it's fair to assume that anything between 15 and 20 per cent of the town's adult population identify as LGBT. It's been a couple of years since my team played at Brighton's Amex Stadium, sculpted so elegantly into the South Downs, but there was a dispiriting familiarity about some of what was being dirged out by away fans. There are some well-worn, lame homophobic slurs in this dismal repertoire, but the favoured ditty of the Neanderthals is 'does your boyfriend know you're here' aimed at the home supporters. I'm pleased to say that the number of such sparkling wits who entertain themselves with this is minimal but am equally displeased that they are not as widely confronted by their fellow supporters as they would be if they engaged in racist abuse.

Magrath's research revealed a kind of split personality among those fans who admitted to participating in such chanting. There are no huge surprises: 'it's just banter; I've got gay friends and I've been on our local Pride march; it's just meant to give your team an advantage'. (Really?) From the dozens of direct quotations from supporters, the one that seems to capture this widespread schizophrenia comes from Bournemouth fan, Kevin: 'These chants aren't meant to offend, and if the gay person was a proper football fan, I think he'd understand that.' If you like, Kevin, but as dim-wittedly offensive as his comments are, and despite the fact that they speak of an enduring prejudice that is tolerated on the terraces, they come from an increasingly marginalised voice.

I Zoom in with Rishi Madlani, who is the campaigns officer for Pride in Football. He's a dyed-in-the-wool Leicester City fan living in London but, in pre-Covid days, a virtual ever-present at Foxes' games. He speaks with energy and enthusiasm about the formation of Foxes Pride some five years ago and how that group has been part of the umbrella organisation of some 40 league clubs working towards making football more inclusive and diverse. We laugh about the fact that his time-consuming, but enjoyable, work in building this inclusivity has turned football, which should be his treasured release from his day job in banking, into another sort of job. It's all worth it, he reckons, when he looks at how football has begun to recognise the need to become more diverse and open.

Rishi is particularly proud of the role played by two of Leicester's young stars, James Maddison and Ben Chilwell, for their outspoken comments on the issue in December 2019. Both young men made it clear that attitudes were changing, with Maddison being adamant that 'if one of our team-mates was to come out and say they were gay, nothing changes'. They were speaking in support of campaigning group Stonewall's Rainbow

Laces campaign, designed to create LGBT-inclusive sports environments which value all individuals. The Laces initiative is one fully supported by Rishi and all the clubs involved in the wider Pride in Football movement. He sees it as part of a growing acceptance and open-mindedness as a whole among those involved in football at all levels.

In terms of how Rishi, his organisation and his campaigning have experienced lockdown, it really is just the same old story. Losing going to football was 'a bit like going cold turkey' with TV being an adequate, but incomplete, substitute. In an echo of everyone to whom I spoke when compiling this book, he bemoans the fact that 'football is nothing without fans'. Part of Pride in Football's approach is to meet with opposition fans wherever possible and although they have made a brave attempt to do so digitally, 'to miss out on your pre-match routines and rituals is all a bit painful', he tells me. When it comes to pondering how to return to going to games, he can say no more than any of us – 'we all want to be back, but we all want to be safe'. We're speaking a few days after the Prime Minister had foxed us all with this:

From October we intend to bring back audiences in stadia and allow conferences and other business events to recommence; again these changes must be done in a Covid-secure way subject to the successful outcome of pilots.

We both find Boris Johnson's statement, so typical of his breezy, evidence-free optimism, entirely baffling. 'Has he ever been to the toilet at a football match?' Rishi asks. All the same, we end our conversation on an optimistic note of our own. Pride in Football will continue to campaign with clubs and supporters in the post-Covid world, working with the FA, community trusts and a range of interested bodies. We both comment on the fact that support for Black Lives Matter goes hand in hand with support for LGBT issues in football. The bigots, we agree, are quick to get on their keyboards when afforded a chance to foment division and it is up to active campaigners to see them put back in their box. In the immediate future, though, Rishi has to go off for his pre-match digital meet as Leicester take on Spurs that afternoon. He is concerned that the Foxes' loss of form now puts their Champions League place in jeopardy. I tell him that he doesn't know he's born. As it happens, he'll have to endure a miserable afternoon and a 3-0 thumping.

In terms of grassroots football, the club most widely known for its LGBT profile is probably Stonewall FC, also based in London. I get in touch with first-team captain Jay Lemonius and we talk about what promises to be an exciting time for the club when the new season gets started. Currently based at the neatly manicured playing fields at Barn Elms in west London, Stonewall are about to relocate right across the capital next to the Olympic Park at Stratford. Having launched a partnership with Adidas and now ensconced in the Middlesex County Premier Division, Jay sees this as an opportunity for the club to fulfil one of its principal ambitions of acting as a hub and example for other LGBT-friendly clubs. 'We want others to learn from us – we're not about pulling the ladder into the loft now that we've achieved something.' The club fields three teams in different leagues in London.

I ask him about the degree of prejudice they encounter when playing and he is happily relaxed about this. As they have progressed through the divisions and more teams have learnt what they are about, the old boneheaded bias is now largely, but not entirely, water under the bridge. He tells me that some casual and temporary Sunday teams in the lower leagues hadn't quite caught up but puts that down to them 'not knowing us'. For the main part, Stonewall wants to forge an identity as a club playing exciting football and holding its own at the highest level possible rather than simply being 'the gay club'. As it happens, Jay tells me there are plenty of 'straight identifiers' who relish playing for them in a 'space that is safe and inclusive'.

When it came to the shock of lockdown, solely in footballing terms, the club, almost uniquely among those in the game to whom I spoke during this period, regarded it almost as something of a blessed relief. Fixtures were piling up as the season drew to an end and availability of players was diminishing. The first team had slipped to tenth in the 15-team Middlesex Premier and in one of their last league games prior to lockdown had been stuffed 6-2 by their friendly, but fierce, rivals, Clapton Community FC, fourth in the table but with little chance of catching title contenders Brentham or Cricklewood Wanderers. Clapton, the 'frivals', warrant a mention of their own.

You know where you stand with Clapton FC: it's there, up in lights, as the main thing you see on a visit to their website. 'Clapton Community FC is an anti-fascist club built on the values of solidarity, cooperation and equality.' Their expectations of those who attach themselves to the club are just as unequivocal: 'we expect, without exception, all our players, members, volunteers and supporters to embody this ethos which will underpin all of our actions going forward'. Jay smiles when he talks of the friendliness between the two clubs but is adamant that, as is often the case when buddies meet on the field of play, this is not replicated when they do so. Nevertheless, he sees both Clapton and Stonewall as 'modern day football clubs who can show that football will not tolerate racism and homophobia'.

Both clubs pride themselves on their community engagement. Clapton have, like so many clubs at all levels, been instrumental in manufacturing face masks to be provided free of charge to local organisations and both are utterly committed to the Black Lives Matter movement. Stonewall will bear the logo on their shirts for the coming season but, as Jay jokes, 'grassroots football can be the wild, wild west and it'll take more than T-shirts to change society'.

But changing society is most definitely part of the agenda in the post-Covid world. Jay talks of the importance of continuing to grow and learn. Above all, in a direct echo of Darrion at Northumberland Park, he talks about ensuring that the club is about building character and encouraging good conduct on and off the pitch. He has no idea what the new season will look like and is unsure about how many people will commit to playing. With their own safety and that of shielding relatives as a concern, the availability that had become a problem prior to lockdown could resurface. For it all, he's broadly optimistic as he works towards building something more than just a football club.

If I thought I was done with Stonewall, I was wrong. Manager Eric Najib has been talking to Jay and insists on contributing. I'm glad he does because I learn a huge amount about LGBT football at grassroots level. He's been manager of the club for 15 years, having started as a player – a goalkeeper – back at the turn of the century. Within moments of speaking to him, it's easy to see why, despite the bad back that's plaguing him, he has become such an eloquent and elegant spokesperson for the club and LGBT football in general. He's been to Downing Street to meet David Cameron and at any number of official functions to promote what Stonewall, along with a growing number of similar clubs, are trying to achieve.

When it comes to that growing number of such clubs, Eric tells me that the current situation is unrecognisable from when he started playing. At that time, for example, one Stonewall regular would travel from Southampton to London to play. Now, he tells me, 'he'd definitely have a local team of his own'. He reckons that there are 'at least 30 or 40 LGBT teams nationally' and that many of them will include straight identifiers. This overall inclusivity is a hallmark of what the club is about. 'We had one of our opponents who wanted to change clubs and told us that he'd like to play for us but assumed you had to be gay to do so,' Eric tells me. 'It's about educating people, challenging people's ideas about gay men and physical contact sports.' He goes on to furnish me with a brilliant provocation.

This is what I say to people about an LGBT-friendly football team. Say you came to watch

us and turned up five minutes late. You'd be
watching a game and seeing 11 footballers against
11 footballers. How would you know anything
about their sexuality?

He makes me laugh about good-natured comments
from years ago, that would now be considered offensive,
from opposition managers and players. Having shaken
hands or even enjoying a beer after the game, they would
express the view that 'you'd never know you were a gay
team by the way you played'. Even the least politically
aware no longer come out with such lines.

I then ask him the $64,000 question: when does he
reckon a current, top-level player will come out? We
talk about how, when it comes to contact sport, the
decision to do so by rugby player Gareth Thomas has
been massively influential but Eric is disappointed that,
like the few footballers who have done so, Thomas made
his decision after retirement. He cites disgraced publicist
Max Clifford who claimed, in 2009, to have two gay
Premier League footballers on his books, both of whom
he advised to 'stay in the closet'. 'For a top player to come
out,' Clifford suggested, 'I would envisage they'd be a
hard man, with an established reputation, and perhaps
a year or two at most left in the game.' Eric's not sure
he's right: 'The first one might turn out to be the poster
boy, with numbers two, three and four following close

behind.' Maybe a more open, tolerant post-Covid world might just encourage such bravery.

We talk about the training that has just resumed in its controlled, distanced way. It's fine at the moment, he reckons, but what'll happen when the weather turns? 'It's all very well asking people to turn up and go home changed, but there are problems.' What happens when someone waltzes off with his kit and he's not playing next week? Do you really want to be getting into your car or on the tube soaking wet and covered in mud? Eric, who works in hospitality, and so now knows a thing or two about improvisation and coping with new systems, admits it's all going to be trial and error. None of it, however, is going to stop him and his colleagues working towards building a football team that has something more to say than simply playing the game on the pitch.

When it comes to making a contribution to that wider, common good, Sarah Kropman takes some beating. She is head of the girls' section at St Albans City FC and a force of nature. She tells me a story of lockdown pathos. St Albans Girls is a sister club to Arsenal Women and one of the perks of this status is that, on a given day during the year, the girls act as escorts and mascots for a game at the Emirates along with receiving some 500 match tickets. As the new year approached, it became clear that the chosen day would

Chris Wood scores a 96th minute penalty to rescue a point for Burnley against Wolves at Turf Moor. The crowd went ... oh, wait a minute.

Swansea hear the news that Forest have imploded and they will make an unlikely appearance in the play-offs.

Fernandinho's juggling act gives away the penalty that means Liverpool are champions.

Out on his doorstep, a socially distanced Liverpool fan enjoys winning something. After all, it so rarely happens.

Keeping the crowd informed at Carrow Road. It was violent conduct and Drmic was sent off – Norwich's second dismissal of the game. They acquired null points post-lockdown.

Don is determined not to miss out on his day at Wembley to see Northampton Town. (He didn't get in.)

Keith Curle cradles the trophy that had to be presented to prove to the full house that Northampton had been promoted.

Gareth Ainsworth searches to find someone to celebrate with as Wycombe seal promotion at an empty Wembley.

Johnny King points to the moon outside Tranmere's Prenton Park. Goodness knows what he'd have made of the maths that relegated his beloved team.

Dale Vince in typically unconventional business attire. The dream of the wooden stadium in League One still on hold.

Solihull Moors' Damson Park looking resplendent under lights. £100 gets you a season ticket there once crowds can come back in.

Adam Hanlon, team leader at Garden House Hospice in Royston, proudly displays his season ticket – reward for his contribution to his community and the Crows' fund-raising efforts.

Northumberland Park Rangers smile for the camera during their voided season.

Stonewall FC shake hands with their 'frivals' Clapton Community prior to being thumped 6-2.

The record is expunged. The Barnet Sunday League wipes the record clean.

St Albans Girls U12s pre-lockdown, but raring to go again.

be sometime in March or April. It never happened, of course, and neither did the visit of the girls' under-8s team to the Arsenal–Spurs derby at nearby Boreham Wood. But if the fates thought they could puncture the enthusiasm and drive of Sarah Kropman and the youth set-up at St Albans, they hadn't been paying attention.

Over 170 girls play football at St Albans City, operating under the umbrella of the Hertfordshire Girls Football Partnership. In early March, as football waited nervously about what to do next, Sarah and the committee met and, prior to any FA directive, pulled all their youth teams – boys and girls – from the games scheduled for the weekend of 7 March. To their great irritation, points were awarded to their opponents, but in a grim justification of their actions, a manager and parent associated with the club were diagnosed with Covid in the days that followed. What also followed as lockdown bit was a period of intense activity as Sarah and her team put together an astonishing menu of activities to keep the girls – all 170 of them on the books – busy and connected to the club.

Despite spending enough time on Zoom doing her day job as a primary-school teacher, Sarah and her colleagues organised online challenges – keepy-uppies, taking on a sibling, quick feet, best celebrations – to engage their charges until some sort of training could resume. There was a 'play at home' syllabus as well as other meet-ups. One of the unexpected benefits of these remote exchanges was the ability of some of the more reticent girls, and especially those with disabilities – a constituency close to everyone's heart at the club – to engage privately and, if they wished, unseen. Another was the ability to hold the annual Presentation Day, numbers for which were usually restricted by the size of the venue, at the end of June. 'One of the parents is a wizard in the IT industry,' Sarah explains, 'and so he set up one of those special log-ins. We had 2,000 people! Grandparents from Australia and New Zealand were all able to attend.'

We speak at the end of July by which time the club has established its own Covid committee to oversee training and the start of a season which has been scheduled for late September. By now, having spoken to her for half an hour, I could not be less surprised to hear of the thorough and systematic way in which this is being approached. Various phases – small group bubbles, contact training with parental consent and the organisation of some friendlies – are all in place. There will be the usual wrangling over pitch availability, but if I were going to back anyone to get it sorted out, it would be Sarah Kropman and her team at St Albans City Girls FC.

People talk about loving the game. When you have the privilege, as I had, of talking to Darrion, Rishi, Jay, Eric and Sarah, that truism comes to life. Reflecting on what

I had heard in these conversations, my overwhelming reaction was one of genuine awe at the energy, time and unbridled enthusiasm they all brought to their voluntary commitments. A former Prime Minister of this country once notoriously expressed the view that there was no such thing as society. I'd have liked her to have met this little gang of people. During a pandemic that had the effect of unsettling us, scaring us and making us fret about an uncertain future, they pushed on regardless, planning to make one aspect of life bearable and for it to be the vehicle for at least a modicum of optimism. They did it, of course, because football is important, but they did it because football, even though it can show itself at its most greedy and bloated at the top level, can bring out the best in all of us.

Barnet Sunday Football League. Premier Division. The evidence has been destroyed and the alphabet takes over. (See pictures section.)

		Played	*Points*	*GD*
1.	Continental	0	0	0
2.	Enfield Athletic	0	0	0
3.	Highgate Albion	0	0	0
4.	Hornsey and Highgate	0	0	0
5.	Muswell Hill	0	0	0
6.	Northumberland Park Rangers	0	0	0
7.	Park Royals	0	0	0
8.	Rising Ballers	0	0	0

Similarly, the records for all teams in Hertfordshire
Girls Football Partnership have been removed from all
online sources.

Middlesex County Football League. Premier Division.
The position at lockdown and the suspension of the season.
Just as well they didn't go for points per game (although
Stonewall's record is simple enough to work out).

Final position		Played	Points	GD
1.	Brentham	18	37	13
2.	Cricklewood Wanderers	21	32	4
3.	Hilltop	15	31	16
4.	Larkspur Rovers	14	28	17
5.	Clapton Community	16	28	10
6.	London Samurai	15	27	10
7.	Pitshanger Dynamo	18	24	0
8.	NW London	14	23	10
9.	Hillingdon	13	19	-5
10.	Stonewall	19	19	-20
11.	Indian Gymkhana Club	17	18	-5
12.	Sporting Hackney	17	17	-11
13.	PFC Victoria London	14	16	-4
14.	Kensington Dragons	14	16	-10
15.	CB Hounslow Utd Reserves	15	4	-25

Chapter 13

Close season. Limbo, vague promises and confusion – and plenty of people trying to do their best

The partially revived version of football that had been in place since late June staggered across the line a couple of weeks into August. The TV companies had carried on bravely trumpeting the apparent importance of games, but once issues of promotion and relegation had been played out to the usual agony of those involved – and, as ever, I speak with some personal involvement here – much of what was on offer lost any sheen. In terms of what football might look like when it returned for the 2020/21 season, we were still guessing, although with every passing day, the possibility of crowds of any sort being in attendance at games was diminishing.

As those of us who watch live football on a regular basis know only too well, the whole business is a clear example of the triumph of hope over experience. We go to games in the hope that this will be the week that our team will sparkle and shine. We do so despite weeks, months, years and even decades of evidence to the contrary. I'm happy to count myself among that constituency. One of the things I absolutely love about it is being in the company of other poor unfortunates and being able to spend most of the day talking absolute, unadulterated nonsense about a whole range of topics. A tried and trusted favourite in our repertoire of drivel is the relationship of the game to TV and, in particular, Sky – although now, of course, a range of other players have entered that particular field of combat.

The way in which the scheduling of games has been arranged to suit the needs of broadcasters is now so firmly stitched into the fabric of the game that it has ceased to be a point at issue. For real-life supporters, the changes to kick-off times at a few weeks' notice is an irritating fact of life, often necessitating changes to work and family arrangements or even, heaven forbid, having to miss the game itself. In the days when we could book trains in advance or steal a hotel deal for the weekend, such plans had to be made with real caution in the knowledge that your fate was in the hands of the broadcasting gods. What was even more galling was that the rescheduling of games to a Monday or Friday evening often seemed to involve choosing clubs that were about as geographically distant as possible, making it impossible for away fans to make such an unscheduled midweek journey. Just watch it on TV – that's what it's there for.

Once this had become a fact of football life, a standing joke emerged that there would come a time when the TV companies would be paying people to attend games in order to generate some noise and atmosphere. Except that it didn't turn out to be a joke at all. In 2018, Rob Wilson, a sports finance specialist at Sheffield Hallam University, produced a report demonstrating that for 18 clubs of the 20 in the Premier League, only 20p in every £1 of revenue was generated by matchday ticket income. Eleven of those clubs would have made a profit even if they had generated no such income. We talk at the end of July and consider how the finances of a post-pandemic game might look as one season ends and another, very different one approaches.

'The impact of Covid,' Rob explains, 'has been to unmask much of what goes on in football's finances,' although much of this will not be news to anyone who has taken a passing interest in football and its relationship with money. Identifying three tiers – the Premier League, the Championship and Leagues One and Two together – he believes that a potentially unintended consequence of lockdown is that it may give some clubs the opportunity to reset and run sustainable businesses, particularly at the lower levels. About the Championship he is less sanguine, dubbing it the 'wild west' of footballing economics: many of us following clubs in the second tier need little reminding of this.

Rob moots the possibility that there may even be an outbreak of pandemic-induced common sense, resulting in the eventual implementation of a couple of measures that have historically been met with vehement resistance within the game – salary caps and restricted squad sizes. For those below the Premier League, these could be lifesavers. Without such measures, more clubs going the same way as Bury will become a certainty, not a possibility: 'I reckon 15 to 20 should be very concerned,' he tells me. Given the leadership style of the EFL, judged by many supporters to be a body characterised by tardiness and prevarication, where would the authority for such important change come from? Would this body have the clout and energy to enforce these potential lifesavers? Both of us are sceptical, but Rob feels that in a post-pandemic football world, particularly in a crowdless situation, a new narrative, and even some structural reform of the league itself, will leave clubs, players, boards and chairmen with little choice.

In terms of the revenue from those attending games, there is no escaping the problems that this will cause for professional clubs in the lower reaches of the pyramid. But up with the elite, TV and streaming will remain the economic driver. We mull over whether the game has been over-exposed in recent weeks and, of course, comment on the drab quality of some games and the obvious lack of commitment from a few teams and their players. Will this tarnish 'the product'? Rob thinks not. For 16- to 24-year-olds, a crucial constituency in the marketing of the global game, the way in which they 'consume' football, flitting between TV, streaming services and highlights on social media, will remain unchanged. The lack of a live crowd may take away some gloss, but this new shared football watching experience, so different from that of old relics like myself, is part of a new normal, predating the pandemic and its effect.

But football couldn't possibly exist without fans in the ground, could it? In August 2018 in a charming – and prescient – observation about Rob's 20 pence in the pound findings, the chair of the Football Supporters' Federation, Malcom Clarke, gave us a quick glimpse into an unwanted future:

> *Players and managers come and go, but we are always there. The reason that they can get lucrative TV deals is because the product shows the crowd, the noise, the away fans and the atmosphere – it is all part of it. On one level they don't need the*

fans because they have got so much money from broadcasters, but at another level they do need fans to keep an attractive product. How boring would it be to watch a Premier League game in an empty stadium?

He couldn't have envisaged the scenario of cardboard cut-outs and flags draped over seats where people should be. But neither could he, or anyone else, have failed to notice how post-lockdown football adapted itself for the TV age, sometimes in unwittingly hilarious ways. Why, for example, did stadium announcers still introduce teams and, even more daftly, substitutions with the same vim and vigour that they would employ in front of packed houses? Why the canned music for goal celebrations – always an inexcusable thing even in the pre-plague era? To be fair, it wasn't quite as daft as players who still insisted on cupping their ears or doing the 'Shhh' gesture at non-existent jeerers and, of course, in the greater scheme of things these were nothing more than minor nuisances. As we all learnt to find our own mechanisms for dealing with a life disrupted in a thousand unwelcome ways, football could hardly be expected to get everything right. And there did seem to be one factor that stood out: for all its clumsiness, football's broadcasters were trying to do their best. As the end of July approached, that was more than could be said of the game's ruling bodies and, much more importantly, the country's government.

The hesitancy so evident in the main media outlets of football's governing bodies was partially excusable – they were, after all, trying to keep a show on the road. That of the government of the day had become beyond risible. On the evening of Sunday, 10 May, the Prime Minister, watched by a record 27 million people, had confused the wits out of people with his 'go to work if you can, but don't if you can't; go on the bus if you can, but don't if you can't' speech. It was the source of dozens of justifiable parodies. He didn't seem to have learnt any lessons by the time he delivered a more low-key and less high-profile address to the nation on Friday, 17 July. Against a background of at least 45,000 Covid-related deaths – the highest in Europe – and a crucially important track-and-trace system that had simply failed to materialise, he baffled us by saying that he was 'pleased to report that we have continued to make steady progress in our collective effort to beat the virus'. Not for the first time, many of us thought that George Orwell, the inventor of the concept of newspeak – government propaganda that showed that black was most certainly white – must have been grinning or spinning in his grave.

When it came to crowds at sporting events, the prospect of some progress was held out and the possibility of 'audiences in stadia' was mooted. The spectre of the disastrous Cheltenham Festival had failed to haunt a government that really should have known better. In a genuine 'can't make it up' moment, Baroness Diana 'Dido' Harding had been made executive chair of the NHS test-and-trace programme back in May. Dido is a busy woman. Before assuming this hugely important position in the fight against the virus, she had been on the board of Cheltenham Race Course and at the time of her appointment also held a place on the board of the Jockey Club. It shouldn't have come as anything of a surprise, then, that following the Prime Minister's speech holding out the possibility of sports events in stadia, one of the three principal pilots for this was to be at a racecourse – the Goodwood Festival. Or, to give it its full, revealing title – the Qatar Goodwood Festival.

'The events,' explained sports minister, Nigel Huddleston, 'have been carefully selected to represent a range of sports and indoor and outdoor spectator environments.' The other two pilots were to be a friendly cricket match at the Oval in London and snooker's World Championship at Sheffield's Crucible Theatre. One of the game's superstars and main attractions, Ronnie O'Sullivan, was unimpressed: 'I don't think there should be any crowds in an indoor area until at least 2021 and, to me, it seems insane that we are even talking about it.' Maybe it was his reluctance to hang about in the Crucible which accounted for his victory in a record 108 minutes in the first round against the unfortunate Thepchaiya Un-Nooh of Thailand. Meanwhile, Huddleston, taking his cue, no doubt, from Boris Johnson's airy promise of a 'significant return to normality ... possibly in time for Christmas' remained stubbornly upbeat. While conceding that while 'not every sport, team or club has the benefit of huge commercial revenue', the fans who help 'keep them going' would look with optimism at the pilots that 'help ensure the safe return of fans to stadia'.

Football's governing bodies remained cautious and tight-lipped. As late as the last week in July, the uncertainty about the shape of the coming season prevailed. A visit to the website of the Premier League yielded no clues about what might happen next. While Sky Sports News confidently trumpeted the start of the new season on 12 September, a search for content for 'Season 20/21' on the Premier League's website only revealed the information that 'the start of the Premier League's 2020/21 season is scheduled to take place on Saturday, 8 August 2020. Details of the fixtures for the 29th campaign will be announced in due course.'

This tardiness on their part was reinforced as discussion continued apace once the season ended. Reporting on the possibility of limited attendances before the end of the calendar year, the BBC was forced into the journalistic compromise of 'understanding' that the Premier League was 'pleased by the proposals and wanted the maximum number of fans allowed back in stadiums as soon as it is safe to do so'. The EFL, possibly caught in a generous frame of mind, expressed the view that the government was beginning to provide 'some clarity' before resorting to its more characteristic corporate gobbledegook: 'We will continue to work with our colleagues [in government] and the wider football family in order to deliver on the timeframe and to assist clubs with the inevitable operational and financial challenges this will bring.'

To be fair to football's governing bodies, when it came to issuing clear information based on authoritative information and advice from the government, they were playing with a shabbily dealt hand. On the same weekend that the Premier League finished, an edict from out of the blue informed anyone on holiday in Spain, from the remotest of the Canary Islands to the centre of Barcelona, that they faced 14 days of quarantine on their return to the UK. Ten days earlier, the nation was told to wear face masks in ... well, some places, but that it wouldn't be mandatory during the intervening period, because ... nope, you've got me there. As for the happy pledge from the Prime Minister and Matt Hancock in mid-May of a 'world class' tracing app that would be 'rolled out nationwide by the end of next week' (news apparently to the team that was developing it, according to the authoritative report compiled by Rowland Manthorpe of Sky News), nobody was naïve enough to fall for that, given what we knew as the evenings, ominously, started getting shorter. With this catastrophic model of leadership from the top, the fact that details for games which looked as though they were going to exist only as TV events for some time was revealed for what it was – an insignificant diversion in the greater scheme of things.

By the start of August, titles had eventually been won and teams had been promoted or relegated. Play-offs had been ground out to the excruciating discomfort of the fans of the clubs involved and the FA Cup had been won in splendid isolation. The two Manchester giants flopped hopelessly within 24 hours as they trundled their resolute way through the European competitions. It made no difference to their chances of qualifying to do it all over again. Any pretence that these cups now existed solely for TV consumption had disappeared completely, as if, when it comes to it, there had ever been anything else at stake as the 'product' sold itself to a global market. Covid had meant there had been no blissful interruptions from football. Wimbledon hadn't taken place, although some golfers had made their way decorously round isolated courses for our entertainment and two brave and welcome cricket teams came from the West Indies and Pakistan to play in sealed, silent bubbles. No sooner, though, had the top two divisions slouched to the finishing line than the whole game, from the Prem to the parks, looked to the middle of September to get going again.

Over on the time-fillers' time-filler that is Sky Sports News, they made a brave attempt to get us interested. A counter on the sidebar indicated that there was only just over two months to go until the end of the transfer window. Irrepressibly gleaming reporters stood outside deserted football grounds, professionally concealing their disappointment that not so much as a delivery driver was going through the glass doors behind them, never mind a stellar signing. The 'Breaking News' rolling at the bottom of the screen informed us that the contract of someone or other may or may not have been renewed. And although the company resolutely displayed an anti-racist message on its news carousel, the presenters' Black Lives Matter badges had, it seemed, been put into cold storage. There was footage from the new Scottish season (Celtic and Rangers both won on the opening day – extraordinary!) which managed to plug the gaps for a few moments, but as the 2020/21 season nervously waited to see if it could start, the current season breathed its last. Was that a collective sigh of relief or just a cold gust of reality that was sweeping over the game? If the globetrotting behaviour of Boli Bolingoli of Celtic, along with that of the members of the Aberdeen team who swanned off drinking together, were anything to go by, it looked as though that cold reality wasn't far away. Scotland's First Minister assumed full-on schoolteacher mode when insisting that their next games be cancelled: 'Consider today the yellow card. The next time it will be the red card because you will leave us with absolutely no choice.' It was an apt reminder, as if we needed it, of the fragility of the times.

Chapter 14

From the parks to the Prem – some kind of action gets under way

Sunday, 16 August. A Sunday morning stroll. And there it is on the air. At first, the sound, momentarily unfamiliar, feels jarring and incongruous – at odds with the morning's tranquillity. Then the instant recall kicks in. It is the unmistakeable, if indistinguishable, barking of men playing football which is gruffly assaulting the ears of the local dog walkers, ramblers and cyclists.

It's a proper game on a full-size pitch, albeit a synthetic one, and so I do what any sensible person does in such circumstances. I stray away from my companions – most of whom are not football people – and I go and watch. It is everything I want it to be. The standard is decent enough, but there's one bloke, rather portlier and more elderly than the rest, who is doubling over trying to catch his breath. There's a proper referee in full kit and, I'm glad to say, he's from the let-the-game-flow school. Man on. Hold it. Turn. Stand him up. No foul, don't dive in. Good head. They're all back. We have organised football. And I'm a sort of spectator, even if it is only for a few minutes before I return to my social obligations.

It had always been my intention to round off my portraits of the clubs at the centre of this book by going to see them live and in action. It was to be both an endpoint to the book and a gateway to the future. However, as we moved through August, the possibilities of doing so became less feasible by the day. I had an early indication of how difficult this was going to be. By a happy coincidence, Royston Town were to play a pre-season friendly against nearby Welwyn Garden City. Thinking that I might be able to use my new-found relationship with senior people at the club and sneak in to see the game, I was informed that besides the playing squad, Royston were to be allowed another four guests. Unsurprisingly, the bloke who nobody had ever seen before but was writing some sort of book wasn't going to be on the doorman's list. A shame; the Crows ran out 4-1 winners.

On the following Tuesday evening, they continued their winning ways with a 2-0 victory at Bedford Town. But while they were doing so, something of even greater significance was taking place. The day before, a group of 30 MPs, headed by Cheryl Gillan and Tracey Crouch (both Conservative) had written to sports minister Nigel Huddleston, expressing their concerns about the future of lower-league football. In doing so, they managed to demonstrate a level of understanding that had eluded many of their colleagues when dealing with Covid-19:

> *Our Non-League football structure across England is football at its purist, often at the heart of our community, rich in diversity and a starting point for many a talented footballer but, unlike League football, cannot rely on broadcast or sponsorship income streams. Their gate and refreshment income streams are vital for financial sustainability even if … crowds are, on average, in the hundreds rather than thousands. Many club gates are in double figures but enough with bar takings to just about sustain the club. Yet the fans returning to support their small local clubs is being considered in the same way as League football clubs, which is incomparable and ultimately unfair.*

Whether they just caught Huddleston at a good moment or whether he was under instructions to throw the public a bone in the middle of the exam results fiasco, their request elicited an immediate, positive response.

He acknowledged without reservation the 'countless examples during the pandemic of football clubs across the country demonstrating their importance to their local area, volunteering both time and money during these difficult times'. The government had been liaising with the FA and the guidance would be immediately altered to allow some spectators to attend games. The website of the Department for Culture, Media and Sport did, indeed, update its advice to inform us of the possibility of this development, taking care to ensure that nobody was yet talking about a return to pre-pandemic arrangements: 'supporters, parents, and other spectators [are] to remain socially distanced whilst attending events. Spectator groups must be restricted to discrete six person gathering limits and spread out, in line with wider government guidance.' While this news was breaking and the Crows were efficiently seeing off Bedford Town's eagles at The Eyrie, I was fortunate enough to be witnessing the community engagement to which Huddleston referred on a sunlit summer's evening at a busy public playing field.

St Albans Girls FC Under-13s (the Under-12s featured in the picture section of this book) are back in full training. Sixteen of them, some resplendent in the yellow shirts of their club but others in the replicas of London's Premier League teams and with three bravely sporting the colours of relegated Watford. Most have made their way independently from a distant car park, but where parents have accompanied them, some incorporating the dog walk as part of the excursion, they are obliged to scan in on a QR code taped to the goalposts. In charge are Paul, Andrew and Ben – the photographer whose own promising playing career was cut short by broken bones in his back: 'The same injury as Neymar,' he tells me, but without perhaps quite the same concerted medical attention and treatment.

All three are either dads of the girls or established clubmen and talk with great pride about what the club's girls' section has built. When it comes to the time he dedicates to the team, Paul is both modest and dismissive. 'What else am I going to do on a Tuesday evening? Sit in and watch *EastEnders*? Ask what's for tea?' He talks of how both he and the girls see themselves as being part of an extended family and, above all, of the level of trust engendered between the volunteers, the players and their parents. 'People trust us with their kids: you don't do better than that,' he tells me proudly. Meanwhile, Andrew has led them on a warm-up run round the pitch: 'Just the one lap tonight, we're being kind to you.' Like all footballers everywhere when faced with this dullest aspect of training, the groaning and grumbling is widespread.

This disappears as Ben leads them in a 'give and go' passing drill, urging accuracy and shouted communication. His charges giggle dutifully when he apologises for his language but excuses himself in the same breath: 'You're all at secondary school now, you'll have heard it all before – you've got to let her know that there's a player up her arse when you pass to her.' The noise ramps up, the skill levels and comfort with the football – the point of the exercise – are obvious. And the extent of the girls' enjoyment, apparent enough while they're engaged in the routines, is even clearer when I get to speak to them.

Alessia talks of her passion for the game and Rebecca talks of how playing football is a great release for her 'stress and anger'! For Olive it's about keeping fit but, above all, being part of the social side of things. For Emily, the best thing in football is scoring a goal, while for Emma, it's about tackling people – 'We've had a few moments, shall we say,' Ben confides in me with a wry smile when I share this with him. As I watch them, immersed in their training and their love of what they're doing, I'm reminded of Eric from Stonewall's comments about walking up to a game and having no idea that I'm watching gay people playing: it simply doesn't cross my mind that it's girls who are having fun; it's just the timeless thing of a bunch of kids with a football. 'Make sure you put us in the book,' they warn me, as I take my leave.

A few days later, exactly a week since I first heard the noise of grassroots football, I fetch up at

Hazelwood Recreation Ground in Palmers Green for Northumberland Park Rangers's pre-season friendly with Akanthou FC. The rudimentary facilities remain closed and so changing and pre-match arrangements take place under the trees that surround the three pitches – all of which are occupied on this mercifully dry morning. I meet Darrion in 3D, as he puts it, and we chat briefly before he goes about his managerial duties. These include thumping a series of balls from halfway as catching practice for the Romanian keeper – 'Watch the hip, Darrion,' his charges cheekily advise. Kenny, an R&B performer of some repute, organises some pre-match drills and sprints. Eddie, a personal trainer who takes these things seriously, is taping a variety of muscles and ligaments before going on to use some sort of battery-operated muscle relaxant on his calves and thighs. A small dog interrupts an earnest tactics talk, and, inevitably, someone has a wee behind the tree. I'm just a touch disappointed that, in true Sunday morning style, nobody is having a last-minute cigarette.

To everyone's relief, the ref arrives. He is decked out immaculately, sporting his full FA accreditation badges but has decided, rather incongruously, to top this off with a black baseball cap. The overall effect is, to be fair, quite striking. His most athletic days are behind him, but he keeps up easily with play and with the firm, no-nonsense approach redolent of the Jamaican parent, his sharp decisions brook no argument. He doesn't even bother with the charade of asking for linesmen volunteers for a friendly. I have, nonetheless, made sure I'm right out of eyeline as a precaution. To enable both teams to use as many players as possible, as well as to build fitness, they have agreed to play three sessions of 30 minutes and so at the end of the first of these, I take the opportunity to speak to him.

I am in the presence of greatness. When he's not refereeing Sunday league football – 'I do it because I love the game' – Kwame MA McPherson is out there winning literary prizes for his varied and original work. Describing himself on his social media profile as an authorpreneur, poet, mentor and orator, Kwame recently became the first Jamaican to win a bursary award for the Bridport Literary Prize and currently has work on sale dealing with the way he has dealt with his own depression. And this seems at odds with the smiling, outgoing and obviously warm-hearted individual with whom I am conversing in the bumpy centre circle of a north London recreation ground. We agree about how good it is to see people back playing football, but Kwame warns of how we need to be 'cognisant that after lockdown, there will be plenty of testosterone and adrenaline flying about'. Certainly, there is no sense of players holding back on the field of play, but, in any case, Kwame's non-negotiable style forestalls any hint of disorder.

Shortly after our conversation, once play has resumed, he awards a penalty to NPR (which is how I now know they refer to themselves). R&B artiste Kenny steps up to hammer it home and complete an accomplished hat-trick. Rumour has it that he may be off to perform in the States at some point and he'd clearly be a loss. However, the summer's recruitment drive has been successful and I congratulate newcomer Richard on the sprint which led to an assist for Kenny's second – 'I did well, because I had a few and a curry last night and it's lying a bit heavy.' He has been recruited via Gumtree. I chat to Drillon, originally from Kosovo, who found NPR on the FA's site. He's hoping to resume his architecture course at Manchester University and is unsure about when he may have access to the campus but is more than happy to have found a team to play for in the interim. 'I met these lads and felt at home straight away.' Still on the pitch is another recent acquisition, Albermarle.

A quick footnote, especially if you're reading this, Albermarle. I couldn't catch up with you at the end of the game – a 4-1 NPR victory – and nobody on the touchline would vouch for the spelling of your forename, so that's my best shot. One thing, however, is beyond dispute: your lightning speed down the wing which led to the first goal and which troubled a very accomplished and tenacious full-back all morning. Given that Darrion had been concerned about numbers when we last spoke,

218

things definitely look on the up – but it's possibly a bit too easy to be seduced into such positive thinking on a bright, August morning of gleaming, green grass and mild, dry weather.

During the game I stroll over to the opposition touchline and chat to Jack, the chairman of Akanthou FC. Like so many of those with high-sounding titles, he immediately tells me that it just means he's the general factotum and go-to man in the running of the club. Akanthou is a village in northern Cyprus and the club was formed as a way of maintaining the links between this geographical origin and those from the area who now live and work in London. Jack informs me of the 'gentlemen's agreement' about the number of non-Greeks who are permitted to play and although I raise an internal eyebrow, I decide that this is neither the time nor place to investigate the politics of quotas or internal Cypriot politics – Akanthou is in the Turkish administrative region of the island. Nearby, Georgina is taking photos for the club's social media feeds and for historical record. She has been doing so for the last four years and doing it, as a glance at the club's Facebook page later reveals, with talent and originality.

Back in Chapter 12, I cited the FA report about 11-a-side footballers identifying high levels of health and happiness. On a pleasant Sunday morning, with six teams of them going to it with a will, as well as the happy groups of supporters of all sorts – earnest coaches, eager kids doing keepy-uppies, subs itching to get on, the occasional weary but dutiful girlfriend – it was easy to see why. A couple of days later, it looked like a bit more of a drudge.

Tranmere Rovers play Preston North End in a pre-season friendly at three o'clock on a Tuesday afternoon. You can tune in and watch it on YouTube. Under normal circumstances, and I honestly intend no disrespect to either side, walking on hot coals would be a more entertaining option. But these times are far from normal. As far as I can discern, the only reason for watching a professional pre-season friendly (unless you're writing a book, of course) is to use the opportunity to go to a ground you wouldn't usually visit – and even as I write that, I concede that for normal people that may not count as a reason at all. On a personal note, I am to be deprived of a visit to Tottenham's new ground which is a shame. Other than a cup draw, I don't envisage Birmingham City going there in the league for some time to come. Still, on an August afternoon that looks more like November, I hunker down to watch an almost game of football.

It's on Preston's streaming service, the information for which tells me that commentary will be provided by Simon Crabtree and Paul McKenna. The latter is a Preston institution who turned out for the club on over

400 occasions. He shares his name with the famed TV hypnotist, one of whose literary works is entitled *I Can Help You Sleep*. I know you'll be ahead of me here, but all he would have had to do was to put you in front of a pre-season friendly between Tranmere Rovers and Preston North End on a wet and windy August afternoon. As it turns out, footballer Paul McKenna isn't present, leaving Simon Crabtree to converse with himself all afternoon. He's nothing if not optimistic: 'Good afternoon and thank you for joining us from wherever in the world you're watching today's game.'

Preston dominate proceedings and although there are few chances, lead by just a single goal from Tom Barkhuizen at half-time. Tranmere's players, who do not yet have shirts with their allocated names and numbers, rally a little in the second half, but after an hour Preston change all 11 players. With a couple of minutes to go, Stefan Payne equalises for Tranmere to the muted appreciation of the few people left paying attention. Simon Crabtree is just about among this number but by now he had to resort to telling us that the first round of the Carabao Cup is on his mum's birthday and that it's still lashing it down. In his post-match interview, manager Mike Jackson, looking damp and bedraggled, reaches straight for the cliché book and talks about giving opponents too much respect but then eventually giving it a right go and getting minutes into legs.

More minutes are put into those limbs a few days later when his team travel to play Burnley. Sort of. The game is played at the Premier League club's Barnfield Training Centre in the grand surroundings of the country house estate of Gawthorpe Hall. While Jacko is trying to get his last-knockings preparation in place for the first competitive game of the season – next week's Carabao Cup game against newly promoted Harrogate Town – Sean Dyche is taking a rather more relaxed approach. As well as putting out one team of 11 against Tranmere, on an adjacent pitch, another is playing Shrewsbury Town. None of the clubs decide that it is worth taking a punt on the fact that anyone will be tuning in to watch a stream and although the goal clips are available on the fans' forums, the response to the games is decidedly muted. On *Up the Clarets!*, in a throwback to early lockdown days, the prevailing topic is still, believe it or not, Brexit.

Tranmere lose 3-0 while Shrewsbury win 2-1 next door. They'll be happy to get the win under their belt. Their own Carabao Cup game, away at Middlesbrough, has been chosen as the season's curtain-raiser by BT Sport at 5.30 on the following Friday so they'll want to be at their fittest and best to entertain the awaiting nation. Burnley, however, will have an extra week's grace. Their season will start a week later than others in the league as their scheduled opponents, Manchester

United, have been granted extra time to prepare following their extended European adventures. Their beleaguered captain, Harry Maguire, may, on reflection, have been better served if he'd stepped straight back into training.

Meanwhile, down on the south coast, a major development takes place as 2,500 Brighton fans are allowed into the Amex to watch the friendly against Chelsea. Sanitised to within an inch of their lives, carrying photo ID and distanced from those around them – even family members – those allowed to re-enter the ground greeted it with unsurprising happiness and optimism. Describing himself as a lifelong season-ticket holder, Dave (he's no Dave Burnley, though) told the BBC that it was 'amazing' and that 'you wouldn't have thought in June that it would have been possible to be back here today, and now you can hope that there'll be more back in October. They've done a great job with all of it.' As the nation waited for its children to go back to school and the government launched its campaign to urge people to return to workplaces, it remained to be seen whether Dave's confidence would be misplaced.

By a happy coincidence in terms of the teams featured in this book, Swansea played Forest Green Rovers on the following Tuesday afternoon. A couple of days earlier, the Swans had been taken apart 7-1 at Southampton in a game of four quarters and multiple changes, but the prevailing view on the forums was, very sensibly, that anyone taking notice of such outcomes wasn't seeing the world through the correct lens. Such calculated indifference seemed to be the order of the day when it came to the FGR game. 'There was a luxury bus at The Liberty with players,' observes owainglyddwr. 'Just wondering if the Swans are playing a friendly today?' 'Forest Green at 1.30. No streams,' is Jasper T's terse response. The home team run out 2-1 winners and even the normally gushing website reports on either side can barely force themselves to squeeze out anything but the most tired and predictable of reports.

Things are a little livelier two days later when I venture to Barnet's Hive complex to watch St Albans Girls play a friendly against the Bees academy team. For those of us with fond memories of the ramshackle wonkiness of the old Underhill ground, The Hive presents its polar opposite. The stadium itself stands formidably square, erect and symmetrical. On a mild evening in early autumn, with the turnstiles firmly closed and the refreshment kiosks shuttered, it is impossible to look at it without seeing a stadium waiting patiently for its lifeblood – spectators – to return. It is surrounded by a set of immaculate 4G pitches and in the early part of the evening, girls and women playing football occupy every available space.

I am pleased to see that as they arrive, the players do what footballers everywhere do when left alone with their mates and a ball. Gone are the drills and exercises: let's practise bendy free kicks, keepy-uppies and new stepovers. Eventually, trainer Paul brings them together, they do some one-touch passing and he briefs them about the game to come. Their opponents will be skilful and well organised, he warns, before reminding them that they're guests at a prestigious venue and to behave accordingly – an instruction that is entirely superfluous given their perfect conduct.

As the game, 30 minutes each way with rolling subs, gets under way, a gathering of a couple of dozen parents and followers gaze through the netting – there are strict footwear restrictions on the pitch itself. Their comments are subdued and decorous apart, of course, from the inevitable embarrassing dad. In the interests of protecting the 12-year-old player rather than her irritating parent – who deserves all he gets – I will maintain anonymity, but quite how this individual thought he was enhancing his daughter's enjoyment or performance through his touchline micromanagement is an utter mystery. Nevertheless, the lights come on – an enduringly magic touch when playing or watching football – but fail to ignite any spark in the St Albans team. They are outplayed by a side that is better organised and possessing more ability – just as Paul predicted. At the end, they touch elbows and pile back into the grown-ups' cars. School tomorrow. Some sort of normality seems increasingly possible.

And that normality seems almost within touching distance on the sunny Saturday afternoon of 5 September when I join a restricted crowd of paying customers to watch Royston Town take on King's Lynn in a friendly at Garden Walk. Numbers have been restricted, but there is still the unmistakeable trail of people making their way to a football match. I meet Alan Barlow, seated by the turnstiles handing out pre-sold season tickets and we chat about how glad we are to be watching a game. My pre-purchased ticket is scanned from my phone and in I go. Whether absence has, indeed, made my foolish old heart grow fonder I'm not prepared to say, but I look upon everything I see as a thing of wonder with which I am glad to be reacquainted.

Outside the clubhouse, the grown-ups nurse pints in plastic glasses. Kids hop impatiently as they wait in the socially distanced queue for Cherry's Burger Bar: 'What's bigger, Dad? A quarter pounder or a half?' No bottles of ketchup or assorted sauces adorn the counter, but there are three lots of sanitiser, one of which squirts voluminously on a startled punter, much to the amusement of all onlookers. The pitch is immaculate and the small stands are freshly painted and postered with Covid warnings. Half the seats are cordoned off but the club could have saved themselves the expense of the tape. In the time-honoured tradition of football at this level, most people choose to stand or lean on railings, occasionally changing vantage points when they feel so inclined. A small knot of King's Lynn supporters occupy one corner of the ground and spend the afternoon doing their level best to compensate for the lack of bar income endured by the Crows in recent months.

On the pitch, their team does them proud. They are newly promoted to the National League – the fifth division – and so, in effect, now two tiers above today's opponents. Although they lost their two fixtures prior to lockdown, they won National League North on a points-per-game calculation, pipping their nearest rivals York City to the title. In January, the two teams had played each other at their home ground, The Walks – not to be confused with Royston's Garden Walk – in front of 4,019 people, running out 1-0 winners. On Boxing Day, over 2,000 had turned up to see them beat localish rivals Boston by the same score. As the game progresses, they look sharper, more skilful and, tellingly, fitter. They run out comfortable 5-1 winners. As I head back to the car, significant numbers of locals head straight to the bar to enjoy a last pint in the fading sunshine. It's a lot more than we could have hoped for a few short weeks ago.

Unfortunately, the day represents a miserable start to the competitive season for this book's featured clubs. Forest Green are beaten, 2-1, by Leyton Orient having gone a goal ahead, Swansea come unstuck, 2-0, at Newport and Tranmere take the lead against Harrogate, only to allow them to equalise within minutes and go on to win the resultant penalty shoot-out, 8-7. I honestly mean no disrespect to the managers of any of the defeated clubs when I say that I am confident that any half-knowledgeable football supporter could have scripted their post-match comments for them. Quite what anyone expects to get from such interviews is beyond me. Nonetheless, in the spirit of welcoming back something comforting and familiar, weary comments about cutting out the errors, making sure we score when we're on top and not being at the races could be deemed just about tolerable in the circumstances.

The days that follow have a dampening effect on any optimism engendered by my sunny afternoon at Garden Walk. The inevitable rise in infection rates as children return to school and other aspects of life as it fumbles towards normality are met by those in authority as if this has occurred as something of a surprise. The accessibility of tests, particularly in virus hotspots, diminishes and never threatens to approach the 'world class status' boast of the Prime Minister, whose overpromising reaches jaw-dropping proportions when he promises a 'moonshot' delivering 10 million tests a day. One of the newly identified geographical areas of concern is Birmingham and, by a rotten twist of fate, a couple of days after I've just watched live football, that's precisely where I'd just received an invitation to watch another game.

In another chat again with Solihull Moors CEO, Darryl Eales, he tells me he has just witnessed his first post-lockdown game – a goalless draw away to Kettering Town. He entertains me with a story about how, with a couple of minutes to go, the announcer at Latimer Park chose to divert himself and others by informing them that 'today's official attendance is … eight'. Darryl invites me to Damson Park for Saturday week's friendly against Hereford where the club is aiming for an experimental crowd of 1,000. His informal invitation is followed by an official email to attend as his guest in the boardroom – and then a lot of things take a turn for the worse, reflecting a growing nervousness about the level of control of the virus. The upshot is that I am unable to go as planned to watch Stonewall in their game against London Titans at Chiswick (won 3-2) and any travel planned for the Solihull area is put very firmly on hold. As autumn approached, it looked as though we were all going to have to learn to cope with unevenness, uncertainty and about the fragility of any planning – particularly where football was concerned.

And in many ways, by the middle of September, in terms of the relationship of football to our broader lives, we weren't a whole lot further on from where we were in the middle of March. As parents who would previously have packed a sniffling child off to school now waited anxiously to locate a Covid test and as millions contemplated unemployment in a labour market where the tectonic plates had shifted within weeks, the game remained, at best, the most important of life's irrelevancies. The EFL predicted losses across its three divisions of £200 million if spectators were not readmitted, at the same time as fantasy sums bounced around the predicted transfers into parts of the Premier League. In a tiresome reflection of its overall policy of suggesting it could deliver far more than was feasible, the Department for Culture, Media and Sport lazily offered up the thought that they knew 'fans and audiences are eager to return, and jobs depend on this too, so work continues around the clock on the moonshot project with the ambition of having audiences back much closer to normal by Christmas, if safe to do so'. A thoroughly depressing visit to the website of the Premier League following its first few fixtures made no mention anywhere of the possibility of crowds returning. After all, you could watch all the goals, clips, interviews and gossip on whatever screen was nearest to you at any given moment across the globe.

It was left, as it was at the start of the pandemic, to players to provide some of the game's best voices. One of these was, again, Burnley captain, Ben Mee. Writing in *The Guardian* prior to his club's first competitive game, he talked of his pride in both leading a Premier League club and of being a part of an institution that was more reliant on values and attitudes than the spending of large sums of money.

Most of his commentary, however, went further than football chat. He recognised the personal difficulties encountered by players during the pandemic and made reference to his own challenge of being the parent of a very premature child born during the period. He acknowledged the enormous contribution to their communities of clubs at all levels and of the part played, often quietly and anonymously, by his fellow players. Of course, he'd like fans back in grounds as soon as possible, not least because it might help drown out the soundtrack from his demanding gaffer: 'you can hear him on TV, so imagine what it is like for us players'. But it is his own response to Black Lives Matter and the aeroplane banner incident that seems to give him as much satisfaction as anything. He talks of the importance of taking the knee, of the widespread support prompted by his actions and his reflection on the entire episode. 'I have spent plenty of time analysing what I said to ascertain if I could have made my message clearer or articulated myself better,' he tells the newspaper, 'but sometimes maybe off the cuff is the best way to do things.'

It might not be the best approach for Prime Ministers and their advisers, Ben, but you did yourself – and football – proud as it stumbled into the unknown.

From the Prem to the parks. Are we nearly there yet? Here are the football results at mid-September

Burnley – Premier League
No competitive football

Swansea – Championship
Newport County 2   Swansea City 0 (EFL Cup)
Preston North End 0   Swansea City 1 (Championship)

Forest Green Rovers – League Two
FGR 1   Leyton Orient 2 (EFL Cup)
Exeter City 3   FGR 2 (EFL Trophy)
Bolton Wanderers 0   FGR 1 (League Two)

Tranmere Rovers (now League Two)
Tranmere 1   Harrogate Town 1   Lost 8-7 on
                                    penalties (EFL Cup)
Port Vale 0   Tranmere Rovers 0   Lost 4-3 on
                                    penalties (EFL Trophy)
Mansfield Town 0   Tranmere Rovers 0 (League Two)

Solihull Moors – National League
No competitive football

**Royston Town – Southern League Central
Premier Division**
Royston Town 6   Newmarket Town 0 (FA Cup)

**Northumberland Park Rangers – Barnet Sunday League
Premier Division**
No competitive football

Stonewall FC – Middlesex Premier County Division
No competitive football

St Albans Girls Under-13s – Hertfordshire Girls Football Partnership
No competitive football – but Emma's eagerly awaiting that first tackle.

Chapter 15

So, how important was it? And could football really make our world a better place?

This book has tried to paint a picture of the part football played in a society that found itself wobbling on uneven ground from March 2020. During that period, it was common for people to seek a sense of perspective about what was happening to them, their families, their occupations and their futures. Although issues of wealth, class and race played a significant part in how we experienced the pandemic, particularly in those early, stay-at-home-or-else days, there was something of a common experience across society. There genuinely did seem to be a case of all of us being in this together. As we spoke to neighbours we had studiously ignored for years, we immediately had something to talk about. There was, it seems, such a thing as society and in many ways, we seemed determined to try and revive a spirit of community that had been dormant for some time. In a grim irony, it seemed that those who had directly experienced the Second World War were most at risk of severe infection and death. Nevertheless, it didn't prevent frequent, if misplaced, comparisons with their stoical resilience during that conflict. How useful a comparison did this turn out to be, especially in terms of the part played by football?

On 15 March 1939, Hitler ordered German troops into Czechoslovakia. At that point, notwithstanding Neville Chamberlain's promise of the previous year that he had secured 'peace in our time', war looked inevitable. The records show that football was acutely aware of the danger it faced: after all, the end of the previous world war just over 20 years earlier had ensured that the possibility of disaster had not been expunged from popular consciousness.

At Bolton's Burnden Park, in their first game since the invasion, home team captain Harry Goslin addressed the crowd to tell them that 'we are facing a national emergency. But this danger can be met, if everybody keeps a cool head, and knows what to do. This is something you can't leave to the other fellow, everybody has a share to do.' For his players on the day, his words must have had some effect as they ran out 2-1 winners against Sunderland.

The season played out to its conclusion with Everton winning the league and Portsmouth the FA Cup. The new campaign started as scheduled on 26 August but was abandoned unceremoniously after three games when, on 3 September, war was declared. Once that had happened, many players at all levels began to do the share which Harry Goslin had urged them to undertake. As the war took hold, players joined the Territorial Army and, in time, regular forces. Some served as Bevin Boys – working in coal mines – and a great many saw active service. Some were rescued from the hellhole of Dunkirk. Some signed up as policemen or auxiliary firemen, some were killed in action overseas. On 10 July 1940, the German air force, the Luftwaffe, began the bombing campaign which came to be known as the Blitz. Houses, schools and public buildings were targeted while private citizens took shelter and feared for their lives.

Football carried on. Sort of. There was a series of friendlies, an attempt to keep regional leagues going, a War Cup and even some unofficial international games. A few weeks after the start of the Blitz, Prime Minister Winston Churchill lifted the ban on recreational football so that the possibility existed of scrabbling through the rubble that once was your house to dig out some kit and get out and kick a football. The Luftwaffe carried out 127 major raids on British cities until May 1942. Some two million houses were destroyed, 60,000 civilians were killed and a further 87,000 injured. London bore the brunt of these casualties with 71 of the attacks being directed there.

One of the main reasons that comparisons between the threat of Covid and the Nazis is imperfect is the nature of those two enemies. Although the latter terrorised the population with frightening air raids, there was, regrettably, something to see, hear and identify. When it came to Covid, it was invisible, its movements barely understood and the means of combatting it underwent developments that shifted by the day and, sometimes, as an increasingly bewildered government screeched from one U-turn to the next, by the hour. When it came to football, any similarity fades completely.

To make an obvious point, but one that is not intended as cheap or demeaning to the modern footballer, the experience of the players could not have been more different. Tommy Lawton was 19 years old when war was declared. He had already played for England and his place was assured in Everton's team as a dashing centre-forward. Such prominence had no bearing on his reaction to the outbreak of war:

> *Then came the war and, with it, the end of my career or so I felt. Surely there couldn't be room for*

a professional footballer in a world gone crazy? I, of course, being a young, fit man of approaching twenty would go into the services. Meanwhile, in the leisure time I had left I wound up my personal affairs, cursed Hitler and all his rats and occasionally sat down to think of what had been and what might have been.

As it happens, it was far from the end of his career and when football resumed in the new normal of its day, he continued to play at the top level for another ten years. Another player who went on to make a handful of appearances for England after the war, Len Shackleton, became a Bevin Boy. He later wrote of the descent into the pit in a 'torture box', deriding those who thought that such a journey might be akin to a ride in a department store lift. He described the 'terrifying experience [of] being suspended on a piece of elastic – one minute you are rushing into the bowels of the earth, imagining Brisbane to be the next stop; the next minute you stop and … just dangle'.

When it came to Harry Goslin, he of the inspirational pre-match address at Bolton, to say that he walked the walk is an understatement that does him a huge disservice. In France, just over a year after the game against Sunderland, he was instrumental in the destruction of four German Panzer tanks and was promoted to lieutenant as a consequence. 1943 saw him serving in Kirkuk, north of Baghdad, where, along with future England international, Don Howe, he played for the English army against the Polish army (the score is unrecorded). A few months later, he was killed in action in Italy at the age of 34. There is no full record of the number of professional footballers who were killed or injured in service and I reiterate the point that none of this is to belittle their modern counterparts caught up in Covid-19 – many of them did highly creditable work in their communities and beyond. Nevertheless, the level of sacrifice of those who served in this way makes comparison unreasonable.

When it came to another principal feature of post-lockdown football, that of crowds in attendance, the situations were just as different. At the start of the war, with regionalised games filling the void, there was an attempt to restrict all crowds to 15,000. In an echo of people stampeding to beaches in 2020, these restrictions were never properly enforced and when West Ham played Blackpool in the first wartime cup final at Wembley – and won 1-0 – over 42,000 turned up. A year later, with the Blitz in full force, 60,000 went to see Arsenal draw with Preston, anxiously peering into the skies, no doubt, in case of an impromptu Luftwaffe daytime raid. Across London, Arsenal's home ground, Highbury, was commandeered as an Air Raid Patrol

Centre. Half a dozen other grounds across the country suffered severe damage in raids.

Nevertheless, what does seem clear, even at a distance of eight decades, is that the determination to keep some sort of football going acts as a sign that its part in public life remains central and important. Quite why this is the case is beyond any layman's interpretation I can offer, but it is telling that in his massively authoritative volume *The Game of Our Lives: the Making and Meaning of English Football*, David Goldblatt contents himself with the observation that in any future histories of modern Britain, he is 'sure that football will play a larger part than in any other earlier era'. Globalisation, TV money, advertising and gambling will all feed into this importance. At the elite level, the game will fluidly adapt to the space in which it is contained. The possibilities of TV-driven super leagues and international club competitions, once the idle chat of grumpy old traditionalists or, more importantly, the fantasy of the console generation, seems somehow more likely as the sanitised, canned crowd noise of post-lockdown football normalises itself through familiarity.

In a way, the actions of this elite tells us nothing about football in a post-Covid world. Nearly everyone to whom I spoke when writing this book, whether or not their comments have been included, was confident about one thing: football at the highest level would probably be able to look after itself and find a way to thrive. That might not be the same in the Championship which shows every indication that it could yet buckle under its own clumsy mismanagement of its finances. And even those sitting in apparent comfort in the Premier League may yet feel the cold wind of geopolitical change as sponsors from China and the Gulf states reassess their place in an increasingly volatile world.

What will not change, however, and this shines through those chapters which look at life away from the high-level glamour, is the appeal of playing football at the best level possible and being part of teams and communities with local affiliations, loyalty and traditions. Whether there is still an overstretched cord that might, just might, maintain a connection between the semi-pros of Royston Town to the glitterati in the Prem seems increasingly unbelievable. But whether a spectacular goal at Bullsmoor Lane for Northumberland Park Rangers means as much to the scorer as it does to any player at any level is beyond dispute.

I honestly make no judgement about the fact that when it came to writing this book, attempts at communicating with those at the higher levels of the game, as well as those organisations that represent them and are their public face, usually came to nothing. Like all large commercial organisations, they had a list of obligations, many of which shifted by the day. The contrast, however, with most of those lower down the pyramid was telling. When it came to Zooming and phone calls, my only function was to sit back and listen as they told me about their achievements, plans and ambitions. I make no apology for sounding corny here because what I am about to say is a copper-bottomed truth: what they had in common was an enduring love of the game and what it can do for people. Although time and circumstance prevented me from seeing most of them in full, competitive action, the invitations to do so were offered unprompted and with obvious sincerity. That I didn't manage to see all of them prior to publication is a matter of regret and one which will be rectified in the coming months. I hope.

And hope is what's on offer. Whether we're in the second wave of Covid-19 or a muted continuation of the first remains a matter of dispute. We all live in hope of vaccines and more refined treatments. By the time you read this, there may even be something resembling a reliable track-and-trace system in place to enable us to lead a more relaxed, less fearful life. We have to hope, too, that the consideration of the needs of others, so evident during the early days of the lockdown, doesn't fade away as the daily grind reasserts itself. The football clubs and the people connected with them featured in these pages show that they can play a part in ensuring this doesn't happen. Those players at the highest level who have spoken out about injustice can be role models for their comments and actions beyond the field of play. The sterling work done in their communities by so many clubs can only be a positive contribution to a society made more thoughtful by what we have endured for a few months.

And we know why football has a part to play in all of this.

Because it's important.

Author's note

The bulk of this book was written between May and early August 2020. There was always an element of running to keep up as I tried to paint a picture of events unfolding in an uncertain world. I am only too aware of the fact that by the time this appears in print, it may already be covered by the dust of unfolding historical and political events. In my defence, all I can say is that I have tried to do what I stated at the start of the book – capture football's place in an unrecognisable new world.

On rereading what I've written, I can see that my comment in the preface about not aspiring to political neutrality has been entirely fulfilled. I make no apology for that. Like every fair-minded person, whether they voted for Boris Johnson and his party or not, I am more than prepared to concede that they were dealt a very bad hand indeed. That they played it with such unremitting carelessness and continued to do so in the face of advice, experience and knowledge became more inexcusable with every passing day. If you disagree, my email address is on page 254 and you can tell me why. As ever, one rule applies: only write down what you would say to my face.

Above everything else, this book could not have been written without the contribution of all of those who gave their time to speak to me. Goodness only knows what personal information Zoom and other online giants have harvested about me and whether or not some peculiar algorithmic profile has been constructed on the back of this. I don't care because it has been worth it to speak to so many people who are simply in love with football and who, in so many instances, are prepared to dedicate their time and energy so that others will be able to enjoy the game as well. My heartfelt gratitude goes to all of you.

As is clear from Chapter 14, my original plan, hatched in May, of rounding off the book by going to see first matches in real action became more unrealistic as time passed. Nevertheless, I reiterate my thanks to all those who invited me and hope to fulfil the promise of making contact as soon as possible. I owe you and I wish you well.

Many of you told me you'd buy me a pint when we met. It should, of course, be the other way round, but whoever would be paying, what bliss that would be. A drink before the game with people you know and like, an afternoon spent spouting inconsequential hogwash and permission to shout nonsense at the top of your voice if you felt like it. Here's hoping.

Index of teams mentioned

(other than in league tables)

This is Jon Berry's second book about football. In *Hugging Strangers* he charted the lows and lowers of life as a Birmingham City supporter. A retired teacher and now part-time university lecturer, he has also written three books about education and teaching and is a contributor to the educational press. He writes a regular blog on politics and current affairs, squeezing in football wherever he can. You can tell him what you think about his work at nutjon@aol.com – but keep it civil and, wherever possible, clever.